# URBAN LEGENDS

The **TRUTH** Behind All Those
Deliciously Entertaining **MYTHS**
That Are Absolutely, Positively,
100% NOT TRUE

*By*
# RICHARD ROEPER

NEW PAGE BOOKS
A division of The Career Press, Inc.
Franklin Lakes, NJ

**Urban Legends**
Edited by Robert M. Brink
Typeset by Eileen Dow Munson
Cover design by Cheryl Cohan Finbow
Printed in the U.S.A. by Book-mart Press

To order this title, please call toll-free 1-800-CAREER-1 (NJ and Canada: 201-848-0310) to order using VISA or MasterCard, or for further information on books from Career Press.

The Career Press, Inc., 3 Tice Road, PO Box 687,
Franklin Lakes, NJ 07417
**www.careerpress.com**
**www.newpagebooks.com**

**Library of Congress Cataloging-in-Publication Data**
Roeper, Richard
    Urban legends : the truth behind all those delisioulsy entertaining myths that are absolutely, positively, 100% not true! / by Richard Roeper.
        p. cm.
    Originally published : Franklin Lakes, N.J. : Career Press, c1999.
    Included bibliographical references and index.
    ISBN 1-56414-499-2
        1. Urban folklore—United States. 2. United States—Social life and customs. I. Title.
    GR105 .R64 2001
    398.2'091732—dc21                                      2001044246

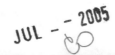

## Acknowledgments

It took me six months to write this book. It also took me 25 years. I've been hearing and telling urban legends for at least a quarter of a century—and I've been lucky enough to know hundreds of people who share my enthusiasm for these wonderful, if completely bogus, stories. Though space considerations prevent me from naming everyone, I would like to thank the following people for their friendship, guidance, support and encouragement as I worked on this book:

My agent, Sheree Bykofsky, and her terrific associate, Janet Rosen; Stacey A. Farkas, Robert M. Brink, and everyone at Career Press/New Page Books for believing in this project; Nigel Wade, Larry Green, Joyce Winnecke, the library staff and the many editors at the *Chicago Sun-Times* who have understood and tolerated my near-obsession with the urban legend as column subject over the years. Special thanks to Steve Huntley, who was my editor on many, many urban legend-related columns.

Much appreciation and gratitude goes to Michelle Carney, who provided an invaluable contribution as a researcher and fact-checker on this book.

Thanks to Lynn and Nick Zona; Bob and Colleen Roeper; Laura Roeper; Laura LeQuesne; John LeQuesne; Sam Saunders; Emily Roeper; Caroline Roeper; Carla Lang; Paige

Smoron; Bill Adee; Neil Steinberg; Phil Rosenthal; Bill Zwecker; Robert Feder; Sherri Gilman; Anita Huslin; Susan Axelrod; Dennis Britton; Carolee Morrison; Bebe Lerner; Julia Wallace; Jenniffer Weigel; Ken Swanborn; Michael Cavoto; Pam Johnson; Rick Kogan; Jim Wiser; Jacqueline Colbert; and Drew Hayes.

Heartfelt appreciation goes to the many colleagues and to the hundreds of readers who have passed along tips about urban legends old and new. I could not have compiled such an extensive collection of urban legends without this ad hoc network of correspondents.

This book is dedicated to my parents, Robert and Margaret Roeper, who believed in the art of storytelling at the dinner table, and whose marriage of more than 40 years proves that love is not an urban myth.

# Contents

# Introduction

Be honest now. What was your reaction the first time you heard about those horrible statements Tommy Hilfiger made on the *Oprah Winfrey Show*? You were stunned and outraged, no doubt. How could such a well-respected designer utter such ignorant, racist comments, on Oprah's show of all places? Serves him right for getting tossed off the set!

You also believed every word of the story, didn't you? Didn't see the show yourself, but you figured it must have happened. That's why you couldn't resist telling your friends.

The problem is, it never happened. When you passed along the gossip about Hilfiger, you were unwittingly feeding the many-headed, insatiable beast known as the modern urban legend. Each retelling of a tale gives the monster another ounce of energy.

No need to apologize. We're all hopeless gossips at heart. The moment we hear a story that's too good to be true (and that's usually because it *is* too good to be true), we log onto our computers, dash for the fax machines, and lunge for the telephones to share the item with a few trusted friends—who then duplicate the sequence with a few more acquaintances, and so on, and so on. Within a matter of hours, a devilishly hatched, anonymously circulated untruth can ricochet around the globe and be absorbed by millions of people, quickly taking root as firm fact and living for years despite all noble efforts to set the record straight.

Modern technology has only served to speed up this process. One school of thought suggested that the Internet, with its power to inform the masses, would help to weed out bogus tales and debunk long-standing myths. What has happened is quite the opposite. The technology that enables a college student in New Zealand to communicate with a high school sophomore in Nebraska, who then passes on the story to a cyberspace pen pal in Tokyo, has put the modern urban legend on fast-forward, zipping around the planet at a breakneck pace. Additionally, the Internet has proved to be a fertile landscape for the endless circulation of phony press releases, doctored documents, concocted quotations and "news stories" falsely attributed to legitimate organizations and/or nonexistent newspapers and wire services. Where it used to take weeks, months, even years for an urban legend to travel around the world (via party conversation, water cooler gossip, and chain letters), it can be a matter of hours before everyone from New York to Honolulu to London to Beijing is familiar with the shocking story of the young man who picked up the attractive woman in a bar and took her back to his hotel room for unprotected sex, only to wake up the next morning to see a chilling message on his bathroom mirror: *Welcome to the wonderful world of AIDS*. (Thought that one was true, too, didn't you? Not so.)

As we enter the millennium, we are supposedly smarter, better informed, and less willing to believe everything we read. But if that's the case, why do millions of people pass on e-mail chain letters and repeat celebrity urban legends without stopping for one moment to consider if there's any truth to what they've heard? Today's information consumer is savvy, jaded, and cynical, yet as willing as ever to believe stories that happened to "my best friend's brother's accountant." The same audience that creates Web sites devoted to urban legends, the same hipsters who chuckle knowingly at the irony-laced references to modern folklore in movies such as *Scream, Scream 2, Dead Man on Campus*, and, of course, *Urban Legend*, excitedly, passionately, stubbornly insist that Keanu Reeves really did get married on the beach in Malibu to media mogul David Geffen, that rocker Marilyn Manson really did play Kevin's best friend on *The Wonder Years*, and that Tommy Hilfiger really made those racist remarks on *The Oprah Winfrey Show*, and we've got to do something about it, dammit!

After you read this book, you'll have intimate knowledge of many of the most popular urban legends in circulation—but you must use this knowledge carefully. Nobody likes a showoff.

For more than a decade, I've been tracking urban legends on a regular basis in my *Chicago Sun-Times* column, which is syndicated by the *New York Times* syndicate to a number of newspapers across the country. Nearly every month, I hear about a new urban legend, or I'm alerted to the resurgence of a classic. Sometimes the reader who contacts me is hip to the game and is alerting me to the latest tall tale making the rounds; but more often I receive heartfelt but woefully misguided "urgent messages" or "hot tips" from readers exhorting me to rush into print the shocking news that AIDS-infected drug addicts are leaving tainted needles in the coin slots of pay phones, or gangs are flashing their headlights at unsuspecting drivers in a deadly initiation rite.

I try to fight the good fight. Every couple of months or so, I pinpoint the particularly popular urban legends making the rounds and I do my best to debunk them via common sense, factual evidence, denials from relevant parties, etc. It's always satisfying to hear from grateful readers who have circulated the column on the Internet or tacked it to the company bulletin board with a note attached that reads: I TOLD YOU GUYS THIS WASN'T TRUE. I like to think I've saved a few people from swallowing and repeating the latest piece of irresistible fiction disguised as fact.

Then again, I can't tell you how many times I've written about an urban legend only to hear from literally hundreds of people who seem to think I've confirmed the story and would like a copy to show to their friends. Sigh.

I've come to believe there are two kinds of people in this world: Those who embrace far too many urban legends (or ULs) as fact and delight in sharing them with everyone in their lives, and those who immediately recognize ULs on sight and would dearly like to read an authoritative, modern work that will assist them in their debunking efforts. A nicely packaged book, like the one you're holding, for example.

This book is for both groups. The aim here is not to mock or belittle anyone for believing even the most preposterous story; heck, I've fallen for a number of them myself over the years, including the disgusting UL about the honeymooners who are victimized by burglars who perform a nasty stunt with the couple's toothbrushes and record it on film. (I still *swear* that happened to my ex-girlfriend's co-worker's friends...well, maybe not.) While it's essentially impossible to completely disprove a UL with 100 percent certainty that it hasn't occurred, I'll come as close as possible to explaining why some of your favorite urban legends just couldn't have taken place anywhere in the real world.

Not that we don't wish that all these stories were true. Think of how much more fun it would be if they were based in reality! It would be fascinating (in an *X-Files* kind of way) to live in a world in which psychics could predict massacres before they occur, Neil Armstrong issued a secret message to his old neighbor when he set foot on the moon, where a ghost is captured on video in *Three Men and a Baby*, and where brides dramatically exit rehearsal dinners after announcing the groom slept with the maid of honor...

But the truth should count for something, shouldn't it?

Chapter One

# THE CLASSICS

No, you won't find the story of the ghostly hitchhiker or the killer with a hook-hand here; those golden oldies have been told and retold in dozens of books about folklore and in hundreds of ancient newspaper and magazine stories. Some of the urban legends included in this chapter do have roots extending back 20 years or more, but many of them were created and gained widespread popularity only in the last few years, and nearly all of them are still believed to be true by many people. For example...

# *"They're stealing our kidneys!"*

A married business traveler fancied himself quite the studmuffin, and every time he went on a trip, he'd seek the company of sexually adventurous young women. After attending a convention in New Orleans, he hit Bourbon Street after a long day of meetings and seminars. Hopping from bar to bar, slugging down potent drinks like Hurricanes and Hand Grenades, the guy got hammered and amorous, determined to stay on the prowl until he found some companionship.

His persistence paid off. Deep into the night, he hooked up with a gorgeous, exotic woman who downed some tequila with him, rubbed her hands all over him, licked his ear, and finally suggested they retreat to his hotel room. The guy figured he was scoring for sure, and he eagerly took her up on the offer. They raced out of the bar and dashed for his hotel, where they proceeded to make out in the elevator like a couple of teenagers on prom night. They stumbled down the hallway and made their way to the guy's room. Once inside, she offered to make him one last drink before they ripped their clothes off.

That's the last thing he remembered. The next morning, he woke up in the bathtub, submerged in ice, freezing to death. A telephone had been placed on a small table next to the tub, and there was a note taped to the wall telling him to call 911 when he awoke. Still dazed, his head pounding and his body aching, the guy managed to pick up the phone. He started to explain what happened, but apparently the operator had heard this story before, because she cut him off and instructed him to slowly, carefully reach behind him to feel if there was a tube protruding from his lower back. To his horror, the man discovered just such a tube. But what did it mean?

"Stay still," the 911 operator told him in a calm, forceful voice. "Paramedics are already on their way. Your kidneys have been stolen."

If all the kidneys that supposedly have been harvested by black market thieves really *were* swiped, there would be a mountain of kidneys piled high in some mysterious warehouse somewhere, and hospitals from New Orleans to New York would be filled with kidney-less victims—but of course that's not the case.

Though these kidney-stealing stories have been circulating for years, I've been unable to uncover one legitimate news account of such an incident, nor are there any medical journals, police reports, or hospital records confirming that the stories have any grounds in reality.

Nevertheless, the kidney-harvesting tale sprouts up like a poisonous mushroom every couple of years, almost invariably in a city that is either a popular tourist stop, such as Las Vegas, or a convention city, such as Atlanta or Chicago.

And Hollywood loves this story. Kidney-swiping storylines have appeared on at least two network series: *The X-Files* and *Law and Order*. In 1999, there was a movie on UPN called "Killer Deal," the story of a cop in the year 2047 who wakes up and learns he¹s signed a $10 million contract with organ harvesters. There's also a weirdly entertaining little 1993 thriller called *Harvest* that used the story as a launching point.

Over the last three years, fliers, faxes, and Internet warnings about gangs of kidney-stealers have periodically popped up all over New Orleans, usually just before the start of the Mardi Gras festivities. Lieutenant Martin Defillo of the New Orleans Police Department told me he's been fielding calls for more than three years. "And still there is no credible information to support [stories of] kidney stealing," he said. "I adamantly believe this is a hoax."

The N.O.P.D. even issued an official notice in an effort to ease the fears of locals and tourists alike. It reads (in part): "The past few months the New Orleans Police Department has received numerous inquiries from corporations and organizations around the United States warning travelers about a well-organized crime ring operating in New Orleans. This information alleges that this ring steals kidneys from travelers after they have been provided alcohol to the point of unconsciousness. After an investigation into these matters, the New Orleans Police Department has found them to be *completely without merit and without foundation*. The warnings...are *fictitious* and may be in violation of criminal statutes concerning the issuance of erroneous and misleading information."

Sometimes, the kidney-stealing urban legend is cloaked in a morality tale, i.e., "This happened to a married guy who let this woman into his hotel room," but just as often the victim is an innocent tourist whose only mistake is letting someone buy him a drink in a bar in a strange town. It's also a neat little chiller of a horror story—the notion that scalpel-wielding amateur surgeons will cut vital organs right out of your body and sell them to desperate patients willing to fork over thousands of dollars—but it's also completely absurd once you follow the story to its inevitable conclusion. If there are hundreds of people stealing kidneys, doesn't that mean there would have to be a number of medical facilities that would accept these ill-gotten organs, and dozens of doctors willing to perform transplants.

According to experts, the process of removing a kidney, transporting it, and successfully placing it in another host is so incredibly complicated that it would be virtually impossible unless a team of highly trained medical experts performed the feat. Tina Weiss, patient services coordinator for the National Kidney Foundation, said, "There is no way this could happen, because the organ donation process is very complex." Weiss explained that in order for a kidney to take, you first have to have a certain kind of match, which is why blood relatives are usually the best possible donors. If a stranger provides a kidney, chances are it won't take, not to mention the immediate escalation of white blood cell counts when foreign tissue is introduced to an immune system, the high risk of infection, and the incredible loss of blood that would occur if someone were to slice into someone's lower back. Our hypothetical stud wouldn't wake up to find a message telling him to call 911—he'd be dead.

Dr. Wendy Brown, chairman of the National Kidney Foundation, said of the kidney story, "It's an urban myth run amok...In truth, transplanting a kidney from a living donor involves numerous tests for compatibility that must be performed before the kidney is removed. It's highly unlikely that a gang could operate in secrecy to recover organs that would be viable for a transplant."

According to the United Network for Organ Sharing, "There is absolutely no evidence of such activity ever occurring in the U.S. or any other industrialized country. While the tale sounds credible enough for many listeners, it has no basis in the reality of organ transplantation."

So what are the odds that some chick in a slinky gown will slip you a mickey, take you back to your hotel room, neatly slice out your kidney, and leave you in a tub of ice? Let's just say you have a better chance of flapping your arms and flying.

UL FOOTNOTE: In 1994, a variation of this story reached Guatemala, where the locals believed rumors that Americans and Europeans were coming to their country to kidnap their children to steal their kidneys. As a result, a number of tourists were actually attacked and beaten by Guatemalans. On March 29, 1994, an American tourist was rushed by a mob who accused her of abducting a Guatemalan boy for the purpose of stealing his internal organs. She was beaten severely, suffering broken arms, internal injuries, severe head trauma, and was in a coma for more than a month.

## Dog swallows cell phone

On Christmas morning, as Lucky, her beloved Labrador retriever, frolics in the background and her favorite carols play on the stereo, a young woman opens a present from her husband: a brand new cellular phone, the smallest and most technologically advanced model on the market. As her excited spouse demonstrates all of the phone's features, she feigns great interest while thinking, "What, no jewelry?" He even charges the phone and programs it for her so she could use it right away.

"That's...great," says the young woman, as she continues unwrapping her gifts.

After all the presents have been opened, she collects the wrapping paper and ribbons for the garbage, and that's when she realizes the phone is missing. She sees the box, the charger, and the owner's manual, but the phone itself can't be found.

"That phone is too small, I've lost it already," she says to her husband.

"Don't worry, we'll find it," he replies, but even after they dump the trash on the ground and sift through it, there's no phone.

"Wait!" cries the husband. "I already programmed *your* new number into *my* cell phone, and I turned on the ringer on your phone, so I'll just dial you up and we'll hear the phone ring and locate it that way."

"You're a genius," says the wife.

The husband takes out his phone and punches up his wife's number, and sure enough, they hear the phone ringing.

"It's coming from somewhere near Lucky," she says, as her dog looks at her with the saddest expression in the world. "He must have buried it in the nativity scene. Look how guilty he looks."

The phone keeps ringing, as her husband digs around under the tree.

"I can't find it," he says.

"I don't understand," says his wife. "I can hear it. It's coming from right under Lucky."

And then it dawns on her husband. He holds his ear to the dog's belly, and his worst fears are confirmed. "Honey," he says. "The phone isn't near Lucky. It's *in* Lucky. He swallowed it."

Needless to say, the poor dog has quite the tummy ache. The wife calls the veterinarian, but in her panic she leaves her new cell phone number instead of their home number, and when the vet calls back, Lucky's stomach rings again.

"Would somebody please answer the dog!" says her husband, trying to make light of things. His wife is not amused.

Eventually they're able to reach the vet, who tells them there's really nothing that can be done other than "allowing Mother Nature to take its course." Later that day, Lucky goes into the backyard and deposits the usual droppings, along with the new cellular phone. Amazingly, it still works!

The *Sun* newspaper in London ran just such a story in late 1997: "Rachel Murray, 27, had left the cell phone under her Christmas tree as a surprise gift for her roommate. But her friend Tony Dangerfield's bloodhound, Charlie, crept into the room and greedily wolfed down the mobile phone, leaving only a pile of torn paper. After a frantic search for the phone, Murray obtained the number from the telephone company, dialed it, and heard muffled ringing from sleeping Charlie's stomach.

"The dog was rushed to a vet, who advised Murray and Dangerfield to let nature take its course. Twenty-four hours later the phone dutifully emerged—in perfect working order."

The tabloid even ran a picture of the gal, the dog, and the phone, which was a fairly large-sized model, about the same size as the woman's hand.

Could a dog swallow a cellular phone? He'd have to be an awfully big dog, and it would have to be an awfully small phone. Maybe if some ferocious beast were able to chew the plastic device down to smaller pieces it could happen, but in that scenario, the phone certainly wouldn't still be working. Even if the world's largest St. Bernard managed to swallow a cell phone whole, how would the phone work its way through the dog's intestinal tract? And even if the world's largest St. Bernard swallowed the world's smallest cellular phone, and it somehow worked its way through the dog's digestive system and was deposited in a big pile in the backyard, who in the world is going to fetch that phone, clean it off, and test it to see if it still works?

My attempts to locate the so-called Ms. Murray and Mr. Dangerfield were unsuccessful. Had I been able to located Ms. Murray, I would have asked her:

1.  If the cellular phone was a gift, how did you manage to charge it so that it would ring? Did you take it out of the box, charge it and then put everything back?

2. Why was the phone turned on?

3. Why did you have to obtain the number from the phone company? If you had signed up your friend to a phone service, wouldn't you have the number?

4. And...did you really want to keep the phone, after all that it had been through?

**UL FOOTNOTE:** The 2001 summer blockbuster "Jurassic Park 3" featured a takeoff on the dog-swallows-phone story. A dinosaur swallows a character¹s phone, which keeps ringing‹thus alerting the characters as to the dino¹s whereabouts. When nature finally takes its course, the humans find themselves knee-deep in dino doo-doo as they search for the phone, which of course is still in working order.

# The truth about Furbys

"Furby" it from me to pass along unsubstantiated rumors about the most popular toy of the 1998 holiday season; my mission is not to spread untruths, but to clear up bogus information.

Several Furby-related stories have been making the rounds. (Say what you will about the Furby, but what urban legends were inspired by Tickle Me Elmo or the Cabbage Patch Kids?) Most of these tales are concocted from pure silliness, but one has a basis in truth, even though that truth springs from a myth.

In December of 1998, the National Security Agency issued an internal memo banning Furbys from its Fort Meade, Maryland headquarters for reasons of, well, national security. As the *Washington Post* reported, "The supersecret spy agency put out a 'Furby Alert' on its internal message system in early December and banned Furbys." The memo reportedly stated, in part: "Personally owned photographic, video and audio recording equipment are prohibited items. This includes toys, such as 'Furbys,' with built-in recorders that repeat the audio with synthesized sound to mimic the original."

In the *Post*'s story, a "Capitol Hill source" said the NSA was worried "that people would take them home and they'd start talking classified."

Sounds crazy, doesn't it? Actually, that part of the story is absolutely true. The NSA did issue that memo, and employees really are prohibited from bringing their Furby friends to work, but the spy agency's information on Furbys is incorrect, as the $30 toys do *not* have the capability of recording anything.

"[The NSA memo] gave us the biggest chuckle," said Lana Simon, director of public relations for Tiger Electronics, the Vernon Hills, Illinois company that manufactures Furbys. "We were amazed that the government apparently didn't test a Furby to see if it records conversations," said Simon. "Nor did anyone from the NSA call us. If they had, we would have explained that Furbys do not have recording devices installed in them. The toys are preprogrammed to speak in English and in a language called 'Furbish.' The way in which you play with the Furby will determine how the Furby will react, but the Furby will not mimic anything you say to it."

Tiger Electronics President, Roger Shiffman, issued a statement: "Although Furby is a clever toy, it does not record or mimic voices...The NSA did not do their homework. Furby is not a spy! You can talk to it until your face turns blue and it will never store a word or kick it back to you at a later date."

The NSA wasn't the only organization that didn't grasp this fundamental fact about the Furby. The *Washington Post* and other news agencies were quick to pounce on the NSA memo as a fun story about government bureaucracy, but as far as I could determine, nobody indicated that the memo wasn't needed because a Furby isn't a tape recorder.

"No, the *Washington Post* didn't call us either," said Simon. "They just ran with [the story]."

In March of 1999, Simon called me with an update. "The saga continues," she said. "Now it's the Navy banning Furbys!" Sure enough, the United States Navy had banned Furbys from restricted areas at the Norfolk, Virginia Naval Shipyard and other Navy bases, claiming that "Furby is a recording device...and a security violation." Tiger Electronics President

Shiffman responded, "Since Furby is so lifelike, it tends to in-spire imaginations. Again, Furby is not a spy."

This is not to say that only government security agencies and newspapers believe Furbys have recording capabilities and/or a "memory" of sorts. Many wild claims have been made about the learning capacity of Furbys, from the woman who swears her Furby speaks Italian to her, to the Furby-files who say their toys can sing opera. (Then there's the phony tales circulating about "rare" Furbys with peculiar markings or black-and-white fur). It all falls under the category of wishful thinking.

And what scares you more: That the National Security Agency couldn't decipher how a Furby works, or that NSA employees were so attached to the toys that a memo banning them had to be issued in the first place?

Of course, the *true* Furby scandal has to do with their fur, which is made from real cat and dog fur. That's right: DNA tests have confirmed this horrible secret. The Humane Society has issued a press release condemning the manufacturer for engaging in such a disgusting and unspeakably cruel technique just to make Furbys seem more "real."

This one is 100 percent false. There's no half-truth or spark of truth, or any hint of the truth here.

"The DNA issue, that one really threw us for a loop," said Simon. "Apparently someone altered a Humane Society press release, but as soon as the real organization found out about it, they issued a statement saying the information was untrue and they were not behind it."

From the Humane Society: "A press release...under the Humane Society of the United States name stated an HSUS investigation found that Furby toys were made with dog and cat fur. We did not issue this press release and want to state very clearly that this information is untrue..."

So Furby fur is made from...what?

"It's 100 percent acrylic," said Simon. "A lot of acrylics were killed in the name of Furbys."

I think the National Security Agency should look into this.

# *Gang initiation rites*

A woman who lived in a posh suburb of Chicago was driving into the city when she saw a car approaching in the outbound lane with its lights off. Concerned about the driver's safety, the woman politely flashed her brights at the oncoming car to let him know his lights weren't on. The driver blinked his lights in gratitude as it passed by, and the woman felt good about doing a small favor for a fellow motorist. She pretty much forgot about the episode until about 10 minutes later, when, on a rather quiet side street, she noticed a car riding her bumper—a car that looked an awful lot like the vehicle she had signaled earlier!

Strangely, the car's lights were once again off. This wasn't right. In the woman's rearview mirror, she could make out the silhouettes of the driver and numerous passengers, all of whom were young black men wearing hats and baseball jackets. Their car stereo was booming so loud she could practically feel it, even though her windows were rolled up. They seemed to be passing around a bottle.

The woman could feel her heart pounding. What had she done wrong? What did these young men want with her?

A moment later, she found out. The car pulled alongside her, and the driver motioned for the woman to roll down her window. Smiling bravely, she cooperated, hoping that the young men wished her no harm; maybe they wanted to tell her she had a busted taillight or a tire that was going flat. But those hopes vanished in a horrific instant, as the rear driver's side window rolled down and one of them pointed a shotgun at the woman, squeezing the trigger before she even had a chance to scream. As the dead woman's car careened into a nearby light pole, the young man in the back seat exchanged high-fives and accepted congratulations from the other punks in the car.

"Your initiation is over," said the driver. "You're now in the gang."

The poor woman, a churchgoing mother of three, had become the latest innocent victim of a gang initiation rite that has been enacted in major urban areas across the country. So whatever you do when you're driving, if you see someone whose lights are off—*ignore it*. Flashing your brights in an effort to play "good samaritan" could get you killed.

The flashing-headlight story has traversed the country like a Radiohead tour, landing everywhere from New York to Los Angeles. When the rumors surfaced in Chicago a few years ago, I contacted a detective in the Gang Crimes Unit of the Chicago Police Department, who laughed and said not only had it never happened, but nearly every element of the story goes against everything police know about the way gangs operate.

"Gang leaders are a lot of things, but they aren't stupid," the detective told me. "The one thing they don't want to do is draw attention to themselves. If they were picking off innocent motorists on highways and streets that are way outside their turf, how long do you think it would be before they'd be put away? Everyone from the mayor to the chief of police on down would make nabbing them a number-one priority. And let's not even talk about all the media coverage something like that would generate."

An exhaustive search of newspaper articles nationwide turned up not one single report of any such crime occurring (although stories about *rumors* of such activity have been around since 1993). That's because as far as anyone has been able to determine, there's never been a gang initiation involving flashing headlights. "They have gang initiations, all right," said the Chicago detective. "What usually happens is that everybody beats the crap out of the new guy. That's the extent of the typical gang initiation."

The big fear over the years has been that some gang will enact the flashing-headlight scenario precisely *because* they've heard the urban legend. As far as I can tell, that hasn't happened yet, but I do know an awful lot of people who refuse to flash their lights at other drivers even as they acknowledge that the story probably isn't true.

Perhaps even more widely known is the gang-initiation ritual involving "pledges" who hide under vehicles at malls and slash the ankles of unsuspecting shoppers. It's only a matter of time before this story appears in a horror movie—the visuals are too sickeningly perfect:

A stylish and attractive young woman drives her BMW to an upscale mall in the suburbs after work. By the time she emerges from the mall, darkness has set in, and she feels just a slight chill of fear as she high-heels it back to her car. She takes out her key chain with the remote alarm; the doors unlock and the headlights flash and the car beeps as she looks around to make sure no one is following her.

All is clear. She puts the bags in the back seat, slams the door shut, opens the driver's door and has one foot already in the vehicle. Suddenly she feels a hand clamped vise-like around her right leg, and a sharp, fiery sensation as the attacker slashes her ankle, causing her to collapse in pain so great she can't even call out for help. The assailant—a wiry teenager—scrambles out from under the car, takes the woman's packages and scampers into the night, the blood gleaming from his switchblade as proof that he has completed the last rite of initiation into his neighborhood gang.

Bulletin board rumors, Internet warnings, faxed "reports," and word-of-mouth gossip about supposed ankle-slashings have appeared in dozens of cities large and small, but once again, there's no factual evidence to confirm this has ever happened, even once. (Not that this stopped advice columnist Abigail Van Buren—Dear Abby—from printing an ankle-slashing rumor in 1992, along with a warning to her readers to be extra-careful when visiting their local malls.)

Although it's not usually stated explicitly, there's a form of racism at work here. The victims in these two urban legends are almost invariably described as "suburban women" (i.e., whites) while the attackers are "inner-city gangbangers," (i.e., young black males). Like many urban legends, these stories prey on the fear some whites have of black gangs. That's the none-too-subtle message behind the "gang initiation" urban legends.

# *Tainted needles*

A woman is driving through a dangerous neighborhood when her cell phone battery conks out right in the middle of an important business call. Her instincts tell her to keep driving until she reaches her office, but she doesn't want her client to think she hung up on him, so she reluctantly pulls into parking lot containing a phone booth. Once inside, she places her call without incident—until she reflexively puts her index finger in the coin slot to see if there's any spare change, and feels a sharp jabbing pain. She withdraws her finger and sees that it's bleeding—and when she peers into the coin slot she discovers to her horror that someone has left a used needle in there!

The poor woman rushes to her doctor, who performs a series of blood tests. A while later, she receives the tragic news: She's HIV-positive.

The needle-in-the-coin-slot story seems to be a fairly new one. I couldn't find any reference to it before the fall of 1998, but in a very short time it has become one of the most frequently repeated stories on the Internet and gossip circuit. However, it could very well be inspired by an old urban legend in which a woman goes shopping at her local department store and feels a "pin prick" while rummaging through a pile of sweaters. The pinprick turns out to be a fatal bite from a viper who arrived with a shipment of goods from Asia. More recently, there have been tales of kids at rave parties or moviegoers who have been stuck by AIDS-tainted needles.

Here's a typical Internet posting of the needle-in-the-coin-slot rumor, dated Nov. 14, 1998:

> "This [message] was sent to me by a very good friend who works for CDC [Center for Disease Control].
>
> "Subject: This is serious! VERY IMPORTANT IN-FORMATION! ALERT! ALERT! FYI...Don't use that telephone.
>
> "There is something new happening that everyone should be aware of. Drug users are now taking their used needles and putting them into the coin return slots of public telephones. People are putting their fingers in to recover coins or just to check to see if anyone left loose change and are getting stuck by needles infected with hepatitis, HIV, and other diseases. This message is posted to make everyone aware of the danger. The change isn't worth it!
>
> "P.S. This information came straight from phone company workers...this did NOT come from hearsay or an urban legend source."

Of course, the sender somehow forgot to include some pertinent details, like the date and location of any such incidents, the names of any victims or phone company sources for the story...little things like that.

Here's another Internet posting:

> "A friend of a friend is currently going through EMT [Emergency Medical Technician] class and they've been warned to be very careful reaching in any slot for return change. I guess the latest 'thing' is placing

hypodermic needles into change-return slots, causing people to get pricked when they reach in for their change. These needles are showing up primarily at public pay phones, but obviously it could spread easily and quickly [to] stamp machines, vending machines, etc. "please be careful. Thanks for your attention."

This hoary tale falls under the broad umbrella of AIDS-fear urban legends. Even if you're living a clean life, so the story goes, you're at risk of contracting this horrible disease simply by using a pay phone and checking for spare change! Is it possible something like this could have happened? Maybe—it's not beyond the realm of possibility to imagine some pathetic idiot or goofball prankster leaving a used needle in a coin slot. It's more likely that the offender would be *inspired* by the story already making the rounds. In fact, that seems to be what happened in 1999 in Wythe County, Virginia, when hypodermic needles were found in post office mail slots, a night deposit box, and a pay telephone slot. The victims in each incident were taken to hospitals and treated, but no one suffered serious injuries or infections.

Wythe County Chief Deputy Sam Viars said that the rash of incidents happened only after the circulation of a pamphlet warning about (at the time, non-existent) episodes of tainted needles being planted in pay phone slots. It appears as if somebody got the idea to cause a scare in the community after reading about what had been only a myth.

In an article in the *Roanoke Times*, Herb Cooley, the police chief of Pulaski, Virginia, said police hadn't determined if the needles found in coin slots in his town had been placed there by a jokester, but he said, "No one is laughing...You hear this stuff about urban legends and people say, 'That never happens here.' Well, now it has happened here."

Copycats aside, 99.9 percent of the stories about tainted needles in coin slots are pure fiction.

## *The Gerber rebate*

In the fall of 1997, I received the following fax at my office at the *Sun-Times,* reproduced here with grammatical tics and awkward phrasing intact.

Reported 8/20/97 (Reuters News Service)

*Gerber Baby Food has lost a class action law suit against them. Gerber has been marketing Gerber has been marketing their baby food as "all natural" but in fact they had used preservatives.*

*Settlement. In the settlement they are responsible for giving every child (under the age of 12) born between 1985 and 1997 a $500 Savings Bond. As part of the settlement Gerber is not responsible for contacting or advertising the settlement in any way whatsoever. If you have or know anyone who has a child born during the timeframe, this will be valuable information to them. Please pass it along.*

*To obtain the bond, send a copy of the child's birth certificate and social security card direct to:*
*Gerber Food*
*Settlement Administration, Infant Litigation*
*P. O. Box 1602*
*Minneapolis, MN 56180*

In another version of the letter, people were advised to send both their e-mail addresses and $2 in order to receive their rebates.

Hundreds of thousands of parents received these faxes and dutifully sent their claims to the post office box number on the fax. Then they waited for their $500 savings bonds.

They're still waiting.

Like many urban legends, this one sprouted from a murky mixture of factual and fictional information. Actually, it was Abbot Laboratories (not Gerber) that was named in a lawsuit alleging baby formula price-fixing from 1980 to 1992. The company agreed to pay rebates of $5 to $45; however, the recipients had to write to a post office box number in Minnesota to make their claim. In fact, it was the same post office box number on the Gerber fax I received.

At about the same time I got that fax, it was also making the rounds through the Chicago school system, where dozens of teachers and administrators were posting it on bulletin boards and sending copies of it home with students so mom and dad could get the rebate that was due. Meanwhile, some companies were inserting copies of the fax in employees' paycheck envelopes. This sort of thing was happening all over the country; at one point Gerber was receiving nearly 20,000 pieces of mail per month, and a similar number of phone inquiries, about the "big rebate."

The company remained remarkably calm through the run of this legend, which still crops up now and then. "We don't believe it's a scam. We think it's just misinformation," said a corporate spokesman.

Gerber also posted an official response on its Web site:

**FREEMONT, MICH.**—Gerber Products Company is not involved in any settlement involving reimbursements to consumers. Rumors that have been circulating for several months involving Gerber and an alleged settlement are completely false.

A settlement was announced in 1996 involving infant formula and pricing issues, but Gerber was not connected with the litigation. The deadline for filing claims under the infant formula settlement expired 1/31/97. It appears that the Gerber name has mistakenly been connected to the Minneapolis P.O. box used to process claims for the infant formula settlement. Gerber was advised by Minneapolis postal authorities that the P.O. box has been closed. It is our belief that the origin of this misinformation is the settlement announced in 1996 that involves infant formula.

It is unfortunate that consumers are being misled by this misinformation. Consumers are cautioned not to send birth records or other information connected with this rumor.

I would agree with Gerber's assertion that this is a myth borne mostly from good intentions. A few people got their facts screwed up and sincerely believed Gerber was offering a $500 rebate, and thousands of well-intentioned (if misinformed) people eagerly shared this news with friends and co-workers. But the company's suggested caution about sending birth records, e-mail addresses, social security numbers, and obviously, cash, to unknown destinations is worth noting. As a spokesman for the Better Business Bureau told me, "If you give out that kind of information, you could become a victim of identity theft." In other words, some con artist can pretend to be you.

Look what happened to Sandra Bullock in *The Net*.

# Craig Shergold's
## dying wish

$L$ike a freckle-faced little boy in a long-running newspaper comic strip, Craig Shergold will never grow up. We won't let him. For the last decade, Craig has been "an eight-year-old boy suffering from terminal cancer," clinging to life while trying to fulfill his dream of making it into the *Guinness Book of World Records* for having the most business cards collected by a single individual.

That's where you come in. All you have to do is send your business card to a P.O. box set up by the Make-A-Wish Foundation (the wonderful organization that tries to make wishes come true for sick children), then pass along the message to all your friends and colleagues, and you can help this poor child achieve his goal before he succumbs to his illness.

Is there a company, a school, or civic organization in the world that hasn't received a chain letter about young Craig? (Sometimes his last name is "Sherford," or "Shelford," but his first name is almost always Craig.) Imagine hundreds upon hundreds of Girl Scout troops, Little League teams, Jaycees, and well-meaning Fortune 500 companies all working hard to collect as many business cards as possible so they can put a smile on that kid's face. You can just see the teams of volunteers carefully packing yet another box of cards and sending it to the Foundation, where some warmhearted administrator will once again be moved by the outpouring of love and affection from those strangers touched by the plight of plucky young Craig Shergold.

Ah, but wipe those tears away, gentle reader, and focus on this: In the real world, if the Make-A-Wish people were granted a wish of their own, it would be that you would *stop sending all those damn business cards to them!*

Not that this is a fairy tale. Amazingly enough, there really is a Craig Shergold. He's from south London, and in 1989, at the age of 10, he was diagnosed as having a rare and terminal brain tumor. And he really did launch a drive to win a place in the *Guinness Book of World Records* by collecting cards—but they were greeting cards, not business cards.

If you check the mammoth 1999 Edition of the *Guinness Book of World Records*, you'll find that Craig achieved his goal:

Here's the best part of the story. In the spring of 1991, the billionaire John Kluge read about Craig's illness and arranged to have him brought to the University of Virginia Hospital. There, a team of skilled neurosurgeons removed nearly all of his tumor, which turned out to be benign. Craig is now in his late teens and in excellent heath as is the urban legend that bears his name.

Somehow, a legitimate drive to collect greeting cards for Craig has morphed into an unstoppable beast of a chain letter. In 1994, the letter circulated through the offices of some of the most prominent business and Hollywood figures in the country, including Donald Trump, Mike Ovitz, Ted Turner, Marvin Davis, and dozens of Fortune 500 CEOs. In 1998, a letter about the business card dreams of "Craig Sherford" made the rounds at newspapers such as the *Chicago Sun-Times*, the *Los Angeles Times* and the *San Francisco Examiner*, as well as the corporate offices of NBA Properties, NHL Enterprises, and the Major League Baseball Players' Association. As usual, the mailing address was for the Make-A-Wish Foundation's branch in Atlanta.

Problem is, there is no office for Make-A-Wish in Atlanta. There *is* a Chicago office, however. When I called them to see if they could "clear up some confusion about this letter going around," the woman on the other end of the line said, "Craig Shergold! Would you please help us with this mess? It's driving us crazy." The Chicago office alone receives about a dozen calls a day on this subject—they've even set up a permanent message about Craig Shergold on their voice-mail system. (Call the national office at 1-800-722-9474 and they'll connect you to the message.) Said Steve Cohen, national president of Make-A-Wish: "Our office continues to receive thousands of phone calls [about Craig Shergold] every month, diverting our staff time and resources from our mission."

In other words, the time wasted on this urban legend could be devoted to helping little Johnny or little Mindy get to Disney World. Mention that the next time some clown comes to you with a plea to help perpetually eight-year-old Craig gather the world's largest collection of business cards.

# "Are you Gay?"

Provided the flight isn't completely booked, airline employees are often allowed to hitch a free ride on their company's planes. It's one of the perks of the job. An employee for USAir—a man who happened to have the last name of Gay—boarded a plane on one of these free-flight deals, but when he arrived at his assigned seat, another passenger was already settled in. Not wanting to cause any problems, Mr. Gay took a different seat.

What Mr. Gay did not know was that another USAir carrier heading for his destination was experiencing technical problems, which resulted in the cancellation of that particular flight. The passengers on this other flight were being rerouted to Mr. Gay's gate, meaning that the flight was now overbooked, and according to company regulations, he would have to be bumped from the flight in favor of a paying customer.

A flight attendant was given a list containing the names of a handful of passengers who were USAir employees and thus would have to exit the plane. (As you'll recall, Mr. Gay was not sitting in his assigned seat, which had been swiped by an unwitting passenger.) The flight attendant approached the passenger in Mr. Gay's seat and said in a loud voice: "Are you Gay?"

"Excuse me?" said the startled man, as his fellow passengers looked on in amazement.

"We don't have time to argue about this, are you Gay or not?" the flight attendant demanded.

"No!" the man proclaimed.

The flight attendant looked again at her list. "Come on! Are you sure you're not Gay?"

"I don't know what you're talking about," said the man, who was growing ever more flustered.

"I'm going to ask you this one last time before we have a major problem," said the flight attendant. "Are you or are you not Gay?"

At this point the man slumped in his seat and said in a soft voice, "All right, all right. Yes I am. I'm gay."

"Then you have to get off the plane. Let's go," said the flight attendant, grabbing the poor man by the arm.

By this time, the *real* Mr. Gay had become aware of the situation, so he leaped to his feet and said, "You've got the wrong man! I'm Gay!"

With that, a man sitting a few rows back jumped up and said, "I'm gay too, and damn proud of it! What are they going to do, throw us all off the plane? This is discrimination!"

Caught up in the moment, a number of other passengers began to make a ruckus, demanding that all gays be allowed to fly on USAir without fear of discrimination. The poor flight attendant burst into tears while the pilot radioed for security to storm the plane and take control of the situation. When the dust had finally settled, the first gay passenger had been given a pass good for free travel on USAir for an entire year, and the flight attendant was sent home to recover from the traumatic situation. As for Mr. Gay, he quit USAir and found a job with another airline.

This story has supposedly appeared in a number of gay and lesbian publications, but I was unable to find one example of any organization taking it seriously. (Maybe it was inspired by the scene at the end of *In and Out,* where dozens of individuals, including crusty old Wilford Brimley, stand up during the graduation ceremony to proclaim, "I'm gay!") A spokesperson for USAir said, "Of course we have zero tolerance for any kind of discrimination," but added that he'd need specific information (the date of the incident, flight number, etc.) to check into the story. Naturally, I couldn't provide him with such information because there was no such incident.

Why is USAir almost always the airline named in this story? It's not because they have any record of discrimination against gays. Most likely, the airline was mentioned in an early, anonymous fax or Internet posting by some disgruntled employee who thought it would tarnish the company's image.

# *Laptop dangers*

I've seen all those statistics proving that flying on a commercial airline is much safer than driving a car or shooting yourself in the head, but I still get a little worried when I fly—especially when they ask everyone to "turn off all electronic and recording devices." What? My Sony Walkman or little GameBoy can crash a plane? I don't want to hear that!

Likewise, I'm always a bit fearful I'll get into trouble when I turn on my laptop computer. I envision the flight attendants rushing down the aisle as warning lights flash, buzzers ring, and babies start to cry as we lose altitude. *Stop him before he reboots again!*

There are horror stories about people who have seen their computers melt down on flights. See, some international carriers have tray tables laced with magnetic strips; the strips are there so that when you place your tray table in the armrest, it doesn't jiggle around and create a lot of noise. The problem is, the airlines never tell you about this. Unwitting travelers go through their usual routines of placing their laptops on the tables, only to see their hard drives mysteriously corrupted by the magnetized trays. The airlines know what's happening, but they're not going to make it public because they'd be liable for damages. What they've been doing is quietly replacing the magnetized trays with good old-fashioned plastic models. No doubt somebody lost their job over this mess, but so far, the airlines have been able to avoid the negative publicity that would surely be generated if the secret got out.

That's how the myth was told to me in 1998. Some Internet postings even mention a particular airline—Delta-owned Sabena Belgium World—as having the magnetized trays. Supposedly, the new Airbus 340 planes were outfitted with magnetized trays that have been crashing hard drives. The postings advise travelers to place a paper clip on their trays to test them out before turning on their laptops.

This rumor continues to make the rounds, even though it has no basis in fact. "It is indeed a myth," said Betty Moore of Delta's corporate communications staff. "Our trays have no effect on laptop computers."

No airline has ever used magnetized trays—and as long as you've got an okay from the flight crew to turn on your computer, there's nothing to worry about.

Just be careful with that hand-held GameBoy. Lives are at stake!

# "Good luck, Mr. Gorsky"

When Apollo 11 astronaut Neil Armstrong set foot on the moon, he fumbled one of the most famous lines of the 20th century. The plan was for Armstrong to say, "That's one small step for a man, one giant leap for mankind," a poetic statement that would have downplayed the individual glory of the feat and emphasized the victory achieved by all humanity. But Armstrong dropped the "a" from in front of the word "man," which rendered his proclamation essentially meaningless. To say "One small step for man, one giant leap for mankind" is to utter a redundancy, as in this context, "man" and "mankind" are the same thing.

Perhaps it is this gaffe that gave rise to the common belief that Armstrong issued a second and even more cryptic message as he began to leave footprints in the moon dust.

After the "one small step" comment, the communication line between NASA's Mission Control and Armstrong remained open, and they engaged in scientific small-talk as he walked on the moon. At one point Armstrong uttered the mysterious line, "Good luck, Mr. Gorsky," prompting the gang at Mission Control to ask Armstrong for a clarification of the statement. He pretended not to know what they were talking about, and for years afterward, Armstrong feigned ignorance.

Many observers figured Armstrong was addressing a Soviet cosmonaut named Gorsky, but a records check of all Russians involved in that country's space program turns up no one with that name. Others thought Armstrong was making a personal reference to a friend, someone facing a challenge of sorts in his life.

In a way, that theory would be correct. Nearly three decades after he landed on the moon, Armstrong finally revealed the answer to this mystery at a press conference in Florida, when a young reporter who had studied grainy old footage of the historic moment asked the legendary astronaut about the infamous Mr. Gorsky.

Grinning slyly, Armstrong said, "Ah, what the hell. Now that Mr. Gorsky has passed away, I don't think there's any harm in telling the story. And I doubt the brass at NASA can do anything after all these years!"

It seems that when Armstrong was a boy of 10 or 11, he lived next door to a middle-aged couple, the Gorskys. One day, the neighborhood kids were playing baseball in Armstrong's backyard when young Neil hit the ball into the next yard, where it bounced around before coming to rest just beneath the Gorskys' bedroom window. Neil climbed the fence and scampered over to retrieve the ball—and that's when he heard the argument between Mr. and Mrs. Gorsky.

"You want oral sex?" Mrs. Gorsky said with a laugh. "I'll tell you what. You'll get oral sex when the kid next door walks on the moon!"

Many years later, as he took that historic walk on the moon, Neil Armstrong thought of that long-ago promise and, in typically cheeky astronaut fashion, couldn't resist sending a message of good luck to old Mr. Gorsky.

Funny story? Phony story. Study footage of the Apollo 11 moon landing, listen closely to the dialogue, and you'll hear nothing that even remotely resembles a reference to any "Gorsky." A Nexis search yielded hundreds of stories about Neil Armstrong, but nothing about any Florida press conference where the so-called secret was revealed.

Brian Welch, director of media services for NASA, told me, "We've heard that [story], and it never happened. I've gotten several inquiries about it. It struck me as a 'Yeah, sure' story, but I still had the Johnson Space Center scan the transcripts from Apollo 11. There's nothing like that in the transcripts."

Just to triple-check, I studied the transcripts myself. After Armstrong said, "That's one small step for man, one giant leap for mankind," there was a pause of about 30 seconds as he began walking on the moon. His next comment was, "The surface is fine and powdery. I can kick it up loosely with my toe. It does adhere in fine layers, like powdered charcoal, to the sole and sides of my boots. I only go in a small fraction of an inch, maybe an eighth of an inch, but I can see the footprints of my boots and treads in fine, sandy particles," and so on.

I studied pages and pages of transcripts, but there's nothing about a Mr. Gorsky. Armstrong never even says anything like, "I'm on the moon and you're not!"

That's one small step backward for an urban legend, one giant leap for mankind.

**UL FOOTNOTE:** Another NASA-related bit of folklore has to do with the science teacher who was "runner-up" to Christa McAuliffe, the schoolteacher killed in the *Challenger* explosion.

Thousands of instructors applied to become the first teacher in space, but there was never any official second place finisher in the competition. Nevertheless, you'll often see postings like this one on the Internet:

> "I have met at least five people who *swear* that back when the *Challenger* had its fateful flight, *their* teacher was the first runner-up to Christa McAuliff [*sic*], the first teacher in space, who blew up with the Challenger. It's always told as a parable about how sometimes losing is really a blessing. So were there just a ton of teachers who were told they were runners-up?"

Answer: No.

# Exploding flashlights

You can imagine this UL as the opening scene in an action thriller, maybe *Lethal Weapon 17: The Golden Years* starring Mel Gibson and Danny Glover, and their false teeth.

A small bomb has gone off in a building after business hours, and now the cops are on the scene, sifting through the rubble in the darkness. One investigator finds a flashlight, and he flicks it on—triggering another explosion that kills several officers. The device had been booby-trapped by a cop-hating killer.

Except it's not a movie, it's really happening. Or so we're led to believe by the warning that has circulated through police stations and posted on more than a few workplace bulletin boards. It starts off with a lot of official-looking text, but the phrasing itself is laughable, as if a 12-year-old prank artist somewhere was trying hard to sound like a government official.

SUBJECT:    Safety Alert—Secondary Explosive Devices

SOURCE:    HQ Naval Criminal Investigative Services (NCIS), Washington, D.C.

SUMMARY:

There has been a recent increase in the use of flashlights as housings for explosive devices in the United

States and its territories. Essentially, individuals have been booby trapping flashlights and leaving them at crime scenes and bomb and arson scenes. To date, these devices have killed one law enforcement officer and have injured several officers and several civilians. The flashlights are generally metal. The batteries are removed and a small pipe bomb is inserted into the housing. The bomber then rigs the flashlight in one of two ways—either wiring the flashlight to explode when the switch is activated, or setting the bomb to trigger if the device is moved at all. A mag light rigged with an improvised motion switch claimed the life of a Puerto Rican peace officer.

During any crime scene investigation, if a flashlight is discovered, leave said light *alone*. If the owner of the flashlight is discovered, allow the owner to take custody of the flashlight. If no owner can be found, contact the local bomb squad *immediately*. If the bomb squad tries to laugh you off, remind them that ATF has reported finding about 20 of these flashlight bombs in the last year, and tell them you're not going to touch it.

If this makes you nervous or apprehensive, good. If you are nervous and apprehensive about things that you find, then you'll be careful and get home alive with all of your various body parts intact.

SUGGESTED ACTIONS: Share this information with Commanders, First Sergeants, Security Forces and local law enforcement agencies.

I love the part about what to do "if the bomb squad tries to laugh you off." And what's with the "Puerto Rican peace officer?" Is that a lame attempt to give the "warning" extra import so it'll seem more authentic?

Is it possible to place an explosive device in a flashlight? Absolutely. All manners of cylindrical devices can be used to house small pipe bombs. Jerry Singer, a special agent with the Chicago Field Division of the Bureau of Alcohol, Tobacco and Firearms told me, "We don't take anything for granted. Any time agents arrive on a bomb scene, they enter very cautiously, making certain the scene is structurally and environmentally safe, and that there is not a second explosive device present."

"[However], I've never heard of any exploding flashlights."

Until they make *Lethal Weapon 17*, that is.

# *Toothbrush bandits*

After a lavish wedding paid for by their affluent families, a lovely young bride and her groom head from New York to Jamaica for a fabulous honeymoon in a posh resort. For several days they live in a dream world of sumptuous meals, champagne toasts, midnight walks on the beach, and great sex.

"This is the perfect honeymoon," says the bride as she and her new husband head back to the their hotel room after another great day on the beach. But when they arrive at their room, they discover that thieves have broken in and cleaned the place out, taking nearly everything that wasn't nailed down. Their clothes, their jewelry, the souvenirs they'd purchased—all gone.

"They've taken everything!" the groom says as he goes from room to room and closet to closet.

"Well, almost everything," says the tearful bride as she emerges from the bathroom. "I guess they didn't have any need for our toothbrushes—and look on the floor by the nightstand. They left our camera."

The police are summoned and reports are filled out, but the newlyweds know they'll never get their stuff back, nor will their insurance cover the sentimental value of some of the stolen items. They consider cutting short the honeymoon, but why let the theft ruin their vacation? With the help of their credit card company, they're able to get enough cash and credit to buy new clothes and supplies so they can continue with their special romantic holiday, which concludes without further incident.

A week later, they're back in New York when the bride calls her husband at work to tell him the honeymoon shots are back from the photo lab.

"Why don't we have a few friends over for drinks tonight and we'll go through the pictures?" she says, and her husband readily agrees. That night, they're flipping through the photos with a half-dozen of their closest friends who are at least pretending to be interested in the seemingly endless shots of perfect sunsets, aqua-blue water, and colorful Jamaican locals. Suddenly the room grows quiet when the bride comes across several pictures of...

"Those look like two butts!" squeals one of the guests. "And judging by all the hair on 'em, I'd say they're male butts."

"I don't understand," says the bride. "Who took this picture? What's it doing with our honeymoon photos? And what are those, those, *things* sticking out of them?"

"Oh my God," says the groom. "Those are our toothbrushes!"

The bride races to the bathroom and slams the door—and there are the toothbrushes in question, taunting her by their very presence. She barely makes it to the toilet in time before furiously upchucking.

The legend of the Toothbrush Bandits has been told so often I'm surprised some real thieves haven't tried the trick by now, as a tribute to this gross but pretty funny story. This is one UL I believed to be absolutely true when I first heard it in the early 1990s. Because of the grossout factor involved in this story, it's a particular favorite of teenagers.

In the meantime, let's consider some of the factors that make this story so unlikely.

Supposedly, this tale has taken place in the Bahamas, Jamaica, Acapulco, the Cayman Islands, Hawaii, Cozumel, Las Vegas—in short, nearly every place an American couple might choose as a honeymoon destination. That's an awful lot of toothbrushes going into an awful lot of rear ends!

Also, for the story to achieve maximum gross-out potential, the toothbrushes must be inserted bristles-first. I suppose there might be a team of practical joke-loving, exhibitionist, anal-masochist bandits with toothbrush fetishes out there—but then again, maybe not.

You would also think a honeymooning couple would take their camera with them in order to capture the memories of a lifetime—or, upon returning to the room and inspecting the camera, they'd notice that the counter had advanced several numbers, indicating that someone had used it. Barring that, would the average photo lab even develop such pictures?

**UL Footnote:** David Foster Wallace's dense novel *Infinite Jest* features a variation of the toothbrush-bandit story. In the book, a burglar named Don Gately and his partner break into the home of the assistant District Attorney who had put Gately away, and they steal "a coin collection and two antique shotguns." A month later, the attorney receives an envelope containing "two high-pixel Polaroid snapshots, one of big Don Gately and one of his associate, each in a Halloween mask denoting a clown's great good professional cheer, each with his pants down and bent over and each with the handle of one of the couple's toothbrushes protruding from his bottom."

Now where in the world would the novelist come up with an anecdote like that?

**UL Footnote #2**: In the summer of 2001, one of the contestants on "Big Brother 2" pulled a variation on the "bandit" UL when she used a rival¹s toothbrush to clean the toilet bowl‹butthe would-be victim was alerted before he used it again.

# *Legends of Rolling Rock*

One of the best (and one of the worst) things about drinking beer is that it makes matters of niggling significance take on added importance.

Such as label fascination.

The more beers you consume, the more interested you become in the can or bottle on the table in front of you. Look at that marvelously ornate design and the exquisite detail of the Budweiser logo. What's the significance of the various creatures and humans on the Old Style can? Turn this empty bottle of Red Dog upside down, and watch how the dog's face turns into the image of a man and woman engaged in an intimate act.

Those were not random examples. I've actually had deep and meaningful conversations about each of the above topics. (And people ask why I've never been married.) Some breweries are quite hip to this label-fascination thing. For example, take a look at bottles of Miller Genuine Draft, which have bizarre and provocative black-and-white photos on the insides of the labels, which means they come into focus only after you've downed most of the product. What purpose do those photos serve other than to arouse the curiosity of the Miller drinker and entice him or her to order another to see if a different image appears on the inside?

For sheer intrigue however, nothing matches the long-running speculation about the mysterious "33" that appears on every can and bottle of Rolling Rock beer. It's the stuff of, well, urban legend.

Rolling Rock is brewed in Latrobe, Pennsylvania, a town of about 12,000 situated at the foothills of the Allegheny Mountains. The Latrobe Brewing Company was founded in the late 19th century, was forced to close during Prohibition, and reopened in 1933.

That's it! The brewery reopened in '33, hence the "33" on the labels. At least, that's one explanation you will hear in barrooms—but it's one of the many incorrect theories.

I've also heard that 33 is the number of days between the time a batch is brewed and the time it's bottled. Wrong again.

Does the "33" represent the number of bottles consumed by a legendary bear of a man in western Pennsylvania who celebrated the end of Prohibition by drinking until he nearly died of alcohol consumption? Is 33 the number of German monks who settled in Latrobe in the 1890s and sold their recipe for beer to the brewery's founders? Do 33 employees have a hand in the making of each bottle of Rolling Rock? Is the current version of the beer made with the 33rd version of the original recipe?

No, no, no, and no again.

Even the best and most plausible explanation cannot be confirmed, because the makers of Rolling Rock figured out long ago that mystery sells better than reality. (If you call Latrobe headquarters at 724-537-5546, you can hear "theories about the mystical 33" by pressing 9. But they don't provide the definitive explanation.)

Nonetheless, we offer the following as the best theory.

Beer-drinkers are, for the most part, regular working stiffs devoid of pretense, but for some reason breweries like to pretend they're as snooty and sophisticated as the owners of the world's finest vineyards. Whether we're talking microbrew or mass-produced swill, the cans and bottles will often include some sort of company motto or pledge, along with a short history of the brewery.

And so it is with Rolling Rock. In the late 1930s, they were trying to come up with a mission statement to be painted onto each green glass bottle, and somebody penned the words you still see on every can or bottle to leave the brewery:

> Rolling Rock
> From the glass lined tanks of Old Latrobe
> We tender this premium beer for your enjoyment,
> As a tribute to your good taste
> It comes from the mountain springs to you
> "33"

Take a moment to count the number of words in that pledge. That's right: 33.

But why would they want us to know this number? According to company lore, it was a mistake. Whoever wrote the pledge jotted down "33" to let his bosses know how many words were in the message, and somebody mistakenly included the number in the final design. The company saw no need to destroy thousands of otherwise perfectly good bottles, so they let the error go—and when they saw how the "33" caught on with the drinking public, they decided to make it a permanent part of the logo design.

In a 1997 feature in the *Pittsburgh Tribune-Review*, a number of Rolling Rock managers were asked about the "33" legend, but they all good-naturedly refused to answer—although one fellow did say, "People have guessed the answer. It's out there."

Growing up in Chicago, I'd never even heard of Rolling Rock until I saw *The Deer Hunter*, in which Pennsylvania boys Robert DeNiro, John Savage, and Christopher Walken gush about Rolling Rock at the wedding reception at the beginning of the movie. Since then I've consumed at least a six-pack of Rolling Rock. Maybe even a few more than that.

Hey, if it's good enough for DeNiro, it's good enough for me.

# "Welcome to the world of AIDS"

Other diseases will kill you just as dead, but AIDS is the scariest illness of our times. When the AIDS outbreak hit the United States in the mid-1980s, a flood of misinformation washed over the populace, which gave rise to myriad stories and myths about how one might "catch" the virus. To this day you'll run into ignorant fools who will insist you can get AIDS from a mosquito bite, a kiss, even a toilet seat. I guess the worst-case scenario would be if you were sitting on a toilet seat in a public restroom, exchanging an open-mouthed kiss with someone while a mosquito bites you. Though these claims have no basis in medical reality, try telling that to the fearmongers.

Admittedly, there have been a number of bizarre and horrific real-life stories of "innocent" people who have been infected or were threatened with infection via unconventional and nefarious means, and that has only added credibility to the bogus stories. In Florida, an HIV-positive dentist in Florida transmitted the virus to several of his patients. On a number of occasions, police officers and health care workers have been put at risk by someone with AIDS spitting at them or biting them. The late Elizabeth Glaser, wife of actor Paul Michael Glaser, contracted the virus through a blood transfusion, as did tennis great Arthur Ashe. Though the risk of infection from such scenarios is minuscule, it adds fuel to the claims that you can "catch" AIDS from all sorts of sources.

The fact is, if you don't engage in any high-risk activities such as unprotected sex with multiple strangers or shooting up with a dirty needle, chances are quite good you won't get AIDS; however, there's still that minute but very real possibility you could be victimized by a freak accident or a freaky human. This irrational fear has spawned a number of AIDS-related urban legends, including the widespread tale of the innocent moviegoer who feels a slight pinprick on her leg or back, followed by itching and bleeding; when she examines the wound, she sees that someone has left a sticker on her proclaiming "WELCOME TO THE WORLD OF AIDS." She figures it's just a sick practical joke, until a blood test a few weeks later reveals she's HIV-positive.

"Be careful the next time you go to a cinema," reads a typical warning posted on the Internet. "These people could be anywhere! [This really happened] to a friend of my brother's wife."

Why is it that the teller of the urban legend is always at least two steps removed from the principal in the story? Wouldn't it be refreshing to hear from someone who says, "I know the guy this happened to—it's me! And I have video documentation and medical and police records to back up my story. In fact, I'll be on *Nightline* next Tuesday to tell the whole tale! Make sure you tune in."

Even more popular than the needle-jabbing tale is the UL about the one-night stand gone wrong.

A young woman is devastated after her fiancé calls off their wedding just days in advance. She decides to go on the honeymoon to Jamaica by herself to drown her sorrows. On her final night of vacation, she gets really drunk with a handsome stranger, and they begin to kiss in the bar.

"Spend the night with me," he says. "I know it's sudden, and I know you're not the kind of girl who would normally do something like this, but I have to get on a plane to New York in the morning, and I don't know if I'm ever going to see you again."

She's not herself. The shock from the broken engagement, the pain she's feeling inside, the liquor swirling inside her...in that moment she makes a decision she never would have dreamed of making just a few weeks earlier. She brings him back to the hotel room (where she was supposed to be spending her honeymoon) for a night of wild, carefree, unconventional sex. Never before has she felt so free, so unbridled. She does things with this stranger she never even thought about doing with her ex-fiancé.

In the morning, the woman wakes up alone. She's got a pounding headache from all the drinks and feels a bit guilty about what she did, but she can't help but smile when she replays the great sex of the night before. She rolls over and reaches across the bed, but the stranger is long gone.

No matter. It was just a one-night thing, and well worth it. She feels as if she can go back home and get on with her life.

Just then, the phone rings. It's her former fiancé, calling from the airport back home. He's so glad he tracked her down before she got on a plane, because he wants to join her and make things right. Spending time away from her has convinced him that he made the biggest mistake of his life, and now all he wants to do is make it up to her. If only she'll let him come down, he's sure they can patch things up. They can even get married right there in the tropical paradise.

They talk on the phone for an hour and a half. Finally the young woman allows herself to admit she still loves him. She tells him to get on the next plane for Jamaica.

After she hangs up, she feels a sharp pang of remorse about the previous night's activities. Even though the relationship with her fiancé was technically at an impasse, she feels as if she's betrayed him. But what he doesn't know won't hurt him. Who's ever going to know what happened?

She walks into the bathroom and starts the shower. As she's slipping off her robe she glances at the mirror—and her blood-curdling cry of horror can be heard throughout the hotel. Seems her one-night lover had left behind a message, scrawled with her own lipstick on the mirror: WELCOME TO THE WORLD OF AIDS.

Before the AIDS era, this same story was told often, but then the message on the mirror was WELCOME TO THE WORLD OF SYPHILIS. Wasn't true then, either.

The Center for Disease Control in Atlanta has never been informed of a documented incident of someone getting AIDS from a one-night stand with a seductive sicko.

"There has never been a case like this reported to the CDC," said Kitty Bina, HIV media specialist for the Center. "There is no documentation of such a case."

Bina added that if something like that did occur, it wouldn't *have* to be reported to the CDC, but an extensive review of newspaper and magazine articles yielded no documentation either, even though the story has made the rounds of nearly every major city in the country, and overseas as well. It remains one of the most popular urban legends of modern times, a cautionary tale about one-night stands, and a twisted piece of fiction worthy of a Rod Serling byline.

# *Bozo no-no*

When I was a kid growing up outside Chicago in the 1960s and 1970s, there was no tougher ticket in town than *Bozo's Circus*, a daily, one-hour, locally produced program featuring host Ringmaster Ned and a cadre of clowns including Cookie, Oliver O. Oliver, and the immortal Bozo. A live audience packed the bleachers each day to watch skits, cartoons, circus acts, and bands.

*Bozo's Circus* was the hottest show in town. Couples that didn't even have children would get their names on the waiting list. It was not unheard of to wait three or four years for tickets to see Bozo. The highlight of each show was the "Grand Prize Game," in which two tykes would be selected from the audience to throw Ping-Pong balls into six buckets one at a time. The farther away the bucket, the more difficult the shot and the better the prize. You kept going until you missed, which usually happened by the third or fourth bucket. Ringmaster Ned would drop a silver dollar in Bucket #6 each day until somebody finally made that shot, at which point the crowd would go wild, the kid would get all the silver dollars in the bucket, and Bozo would come out riding the new bicycle that was part of the grand prize package.

As kids, we thought *Bozo's Circus* was unique to Chicago, but dozens of cities had their own version of the circus, just like they had their own local *Romper Room* in the morning. And that's why people all over the country are absolutely sure they witnessed the moment when Bozo got his comeuppance from a smart-aleck kid who had bombed out on the Grand Prize Game.

Seems there was this little troublemaker who was selected to participate in the Grand Prize Game. He was thrilled to make the first two buckets, but when toss number three bounced off the rim, he blurted, "Oh, s#*t!"

The crowd of moms and dads and little kids was stunned silent. Ringmaster Ned didn't know what to say. Clowns and jugglers looked on from the wings in open-mouthed shock. Finally Bozo stepped forward and said, "Now, now, little boy, that's a Bozo no-no."

"Ah, cram it, clownie!" said the boy as he stomped off. They cut to a commercial, and when the show returned, Bozo and Ringmaster Ned gave a talk about curse words and why they're not for children.

A friend of mine who grew up in Baltimore "remembered" the story a bit differently. "There was a game where you had to walk across the room with an egg on a spoon, and if your egg dropped, you were eliminated," she told me. "When this little boy's egg fell off the spoon, he started to cry, so Bozo rushed over and gave him some kind of cheap consolation prize, like a T-shirt or something, and the kid looked up at Bozo and said, 'Why don't you shove your stupid toy, Bozo.' "

The clown in question isn't always named Bozo, either. In some cities they had knockoff versions of *Bozo's Circus*, with the lead clown named Chuckles, or Shakes, or Gary, or whatever. The story is essentially the same.

Weirdly enough, Larry Harmon, who was the original Bozo and who is credited with creating the Bozo franchise, has bought into this urban legend. According to Harmon, it really happened in Boston in the 1960s, though he doesn't have any more evidence than anyone else.

That the story has been told so many times in so many cities is the best evidence that it never happened. However, *Bozo's Circus* was almost always televised live, so it's possible that at some point in some city, some little kid mixed it up with Bozo and uttered an expletive or two. But you'd think such an incident would have at least merited a mention in a local paper somewhere. No such stories have ever been unearthed.

So the next time someone swears to have seen the show in question, remind them that trying to pass off urban legends as fact is a Bozo no-no.

# *Flight 261*
## *stopped in mid-prayer*

If there is a God and if this God has a plan, it's too complex and great for the human mind to comprehend. When a child dies, people say things like, "She's with the angels now," or, "God needed her in heaven," because there is no earthly rationale for such a tragedy.

And so it is with urban legends that speak of miracles that occur in times of great disaster, to wit, the final nine minutes of Flight 261.

The story as it's told is often attributed to that noted purveyor of urban legends, Mr. Paul Harvey, and it goes like this:

"We've some incredible news about the last few minutes of Alaska Airlines Flight 261, before it crashed back in January [2000]. A man related last week that he had talked with an Alaska Airlines pilot involved in the investigation of the crash; this pilot has listened to the cockpit voice recorder from the downed plane, and he reports that during the last nine minutes of the flight, the wife of the pastor from Monroe, Washington, can be heard sharing the Gospel with the passengers over the airplane's intercom system. The pastor and his wife were returning from a missionary trip to Mexico.

"Just before the fatal dive into the Pacific Ocean, she can be heard leading the sinners as they pray for salvation. The pilot also said that the flight data recorder from the plane indicates that there is no good explanation for the plane remaining in the air for those final nine minutes. But it did remain in the air until the pastor's wife finished sharing the Gospel and presumably leading many to Christ in those final moments.

"Interestingly enough, we haven't heard about this on the evening news."

Right. Because television newscasts tend to shy away from spectacularly chilling stories about documented but inexplicable phenomena connected with a deadly plane crash. You wouldn't want to attract tons of viewers or anything.

Here we go again with people spreading a story that slams the godless, liberal media—even though the story itself is highly questionable.

Some facts about the crash of Flight 261:

➤ On Jan. 31, 2000, Alaska Airlines Flight 261 plunged into the Pacific Ocean about 40 miles northwest of Los Angeles, killing all 88 aboard the aircraft.

➤ The cause of the crash has yet to be determined, but the stabilizing system seems to have failed.

➤ Some news reports say that after the plane started to dive, the crew regained control temporarily—for about nine minutes.

➤ Among the passengers on the plane were Joe and Linda Knight, pastors of the Rock Church in Monroe, Washington.

Any assertions beyond that fall into the realm of speculation and rumor. The contents of the cockpit voice recorder, aka the "black box" (which by the way is usually orange, the better to be sighted by investigators after a crash), have not been released to the public, but the transcript of the exchange between the pilot and the air traffic control tower makes no mention of Linda Knight and contains no reference to anyone saying prayers, although the simple declarations from the pilot are chilling enough: "Center Alaska two-sixty-one we are in a dive here...we're in a vertical dive—not a dive yet—but we've lost vertical control of the plane...we've got it back under control there, no we don't..."

Yet within a few weeks of the crash, the Internet was buzzing with rumors about the "Miracle of Flight 261."

My questions are many. Surely not everyone aboard that plane was Christian, or was willing to "come to Christ" in the last nine minutes of that flight, so what did those people do? If God could suspend the plane in mid-air so that Knight could finish praying, why not just restore stability to the flight after everyone had prayed and asked for salvation? Why nine minutes?

Understand, I'm not questioning the faith of the Knights. It's quite possible that they and others spent their final moments praying and asking for salvation. But there's no evidence that any group prayer took place over the intercom, nor is there proof that the plane's descent was affected by some kind of spiritual intervention.

For that matter, Paul Harvey shouldn't take the blame for spreading this story, as he never mentioned it on his radio show.

In April 2000, the *Seattle Post-Intelligencer*'s James Wallace reported on the rumors about Flight 261.

"No one will ever know exactly what happened aboard the flight," wrote Wallace. "But sources close to the federal crash investigation said the cockpit voice recorder did not pick up any final prayer...

"However, in interviews with reporters after the crash, Jeff Knight, the family's son, said he was sure his mother would have been standing in the aisle during the plane's last moments, preaching and helping frightened people find God.

"'A lot of people met Jesus that day through my mom,' he was quoted as saying."

It's not my place to question a son about what he believes happened in his mother's last minutes. But we're talking about what Jeff Knight *believes*, not what he or anyone else knows to be true.

One final twist of fate that is true, according to an article in *People* magazine: The Knights were almost prevented from boarding Flight 261 in Mexico because Joe's passport had expired. But they somehow talked their way onto the flight—a flight that never made it home.

# George Turklebaum, we hardly knew ye

In life, George Turklebaum was a non-descript, Dilbert-type character who achieved nothing remarkable and left no great impression on those who worked with him. For 30 years, Turklebaum toiled anonymously as a proofreader for a large New York firm, keeping to himself and attracting little attention. Most of his co-workers never had a conversation with him that extended beyond, "How's it going, Turklebaum?" or, "Have a nice weekend, Turklebaum."

But in death, George Turklebaum became a folk hero, and a symbol of the struggle, to under appreciated cubicle-dwellers everywhere. Because when Turklebaum died, nobody noticed—for five full days.

The story first appeared in the Guardian and on the BBC, but it was the *Birmingham* (England) *Sunday Mercury* that fleshed out the details and subsequently claimed credit for "breaking" this most unusual tale.

From the Dec. 17, 2000, edition of the *Mercury*:

> Bosses of a publishing firm are trying to work out why no one noticed that one of their employees had been sitting dead at his desk for FIVE DAYS before anyone asked if he was feeling okay.

George Turklebaum, 51, who had been employed as a proofreader at a New York firm for 30 years, had a heart attack in the open-plan office he shared with 23 other workers.

He quietly passed away Monday, but nobody noticed until Saturday morning when an office cleaner asked why he was still working the weekend.

His boss Elliot Wachiaski said: 'George was always the first guy in each morning and the last to leave at night—so no one found it unusual that he was in the same position all that time and didn't say anything.'

An ironic postscript, according to the *Mercury*: George was proofreading medical textbooks when he died of a massive coronary.

A few weeks later the *London Times* picked up on the story, and took a none-too-subtle jab at work habits in the United States.

From New York comes the awful tale of George Turklebaum, a proofreader at a publishing firm there, and quite possibly, the victim of the American long-hours culture...

You'd think the New York tabloids would have jumped all over this story. One can imagine the possible headlines in the Post:

DEAD MAN WORKING

NO O.T. FOR DOA

A REAL WORKING STIFF

Oddly enough, though, none of the New York papers ever reported a word about the demise of Mr. Turklebaum. For that matter, neither the New York telephone books from 2000 nor a database search yielded a single mention of a George Turklebaum—or of an Elliot Wachiaski, the supervisor who supposedly eulogized Turklebaum in the press. Curious, too, is the failure of the original article to name the firm for which ol' Turk worked for all those years.

Not to mention the gaps in logic in this story. It might be possible for someone to doze off for a few hours at his desk without anyone noticing—but are we really to believe that a human being could be slumped over without moving for an entire working week and nobody would notice? Doesn't this firm have a night cleaning crew that comes in to vacuum the carpet and empty the trash and dust the computer terminals? What'd they do, work around poor George?

Besides, the smell from a decomposing corpse would resonate throughout an entire office floor after a couple of days.

Even in the most insulated, isolated, and antiseptic office environment, the kind of place where you don't even know the names of half the people in your department, it would be virtually impossible for a body to go undetected for five full days.

A few weeks before George Turklebaum's death made global news, the anonymous-employee concept was exploited in different fashion by 26-year-old Rodney Rothman, who published a piece in the *New Yorker* titled "My Fake Job." Rothman, a former head writer on *The Late Show with David Letterman*, wrote a brilliant and hilarious account of the 17 days he spent as an employee of a dotcom company in Manhattan—without having actually been hired by the firm.

Rothman took a desk, enjoyed the perk of a free massage, double-talked his way out of tricky situations, and killed time by shooting the breeze with other employees.

"I don't smoke, but I still take a cigarette break every day at four o'clock," wrote Rothman. "I stand there and let the cigarette burn down. I pretend to inhale, lightly, so I don't trigger a coughing fit. The office smokers never notice; they're too busy complaining about their newly worthless stock options, or how the latest reorg left them with a job title they don't even understand, like 'resource manager.' I never speak up, because there is a crucial difference between my colleagues and me: I was never hired to work at this company."

Rothman's article generated terrific buzz and earned him much praise for a hilarious and scathing indictment of an Internet economy booming and careening so quickly and haphazardly that someone could work at a company for two and a half weeks without so much as raising an eyebrow. What a wacky world!

Alas, "My Fake Job" was more than a bit of a fake itself. Employees of Luminant Worldwide in Manhattan recognized enough details in Rothman's piece to determine that the firm in question was their company—and they were quick to pounce on inconsistencies and outright fabrications in his story. The office massage, for example, was pure fiction, as Rothman later admitted to the *New Yorker*. And Rothman had neglected to reveal that he hadn't exactly stumbled into Luminant Worldwide by chance; in fact, his mother worked there.

Editors at the *New Yorker* were none too pleased with Rothman's blending of fact and fiction. Two weeks after his piece appeared, they issued a note:

"We have learned that in his piece 'My Fake Job' (Nov. 27), Rodney Rothman changed identifying details about the workplace and described an incident—a massage at his office, as it happens—that did not take place. Also, the author should have revealed that his mother worked at the company. The magazine does not disguise details or mix fact and fiction without informing the reader (not even in a comic piece like this one), and we sincerely regret the error."

Here at the Urban Legends Home Office, we also wonder if Rothman was a big fan of *Seinfeld*, as his prank reminds us of the episode in which Kramer packed a briefcase, dressed in a business suit, and went to work at an office—even though nobody had hired him.

Chapter Two

# BIG LIES ON CAMPUS

It made sense for the movie *Urban Legend* to take place in and around a college campus, as these institutions of higher learning have long been fertile ground for the launching and retelling of literally dozens of modern myths, most of them covering one of three topics: murder, sex, or cheating on exams.

A college campus is the perfect place for a too-good-to-be-true story to thrive for generations. With a complete turnover of the student population every four or five years, the tale can be passed from one class to another, and in dorm rooms, fraternity, and sorority houses, with the original source long since removed. Many of these stories sound quite plausible, if it weren't for the fact that the same elements of a story will crop up in campuses across the country...

# *Psychic predicts*
## *massacre*

If somebody at Bowling Green State University in Ohio had talked to somebody at the University of San Diego in California in October of 1998, both schools could have avoided a lot of unnecessary panic. Based on the stories sweeping their respective campuses at the time, a conversation between our imaginary students might have gone something like this:

Bowling Green Student:
> You're never going to believe what's happening here! People are freaking out.

San Diego Student:
> You think you're freaking out there, you should see what's going on here! I guarantee you it's crazier than anything happening on your campus. We're in the middle of a major meltdown, I know you can't top that.

BG:    I wouldn't be so sure. It's insane around here.

SD:    OK, I'll go first and then you can tell me your story. There's this psychic guy—he's supposed to be the most famous psychic in the world, he predicted the Oklahoma City bombing—and he went on Oprah Winfrey's show and predicted there was going to be a mass murder on Halloween at an H-shaped residence hall, and guess what, *we* have an H-shaped residence hall at USD...well actually, it's more of an A-shape, but it's close enough, and it's called Camino/Founders Hall, so everybody who lives there is totally losing it and—

BG:     Wait a min—

SD:     Hold on. This psychic predicted the massacre would take place on Halloween, and everybody on campus has been talking about it and people are getting really scared, and there's something like 280 women who live in Camino/Founders Hall and everyone who lives there is clearing out. Camino/Founders is a total ghost town right now.

(There's a long pause)

SD:     What's the matter?

BG:     I don't know what you're talking about, because the psychic who was on *Oprah* didn't say anything about an H-shaped building. He said the massacre was going to take place at a state college in the Midwest and he even mentioned Bowling Green as one of the possibilities, and that's why people are freaking out here!

SD:     I don't get it. Did you see the show when the guy was on?

BG:     Um, no. Did you?

SD:     No, I didn't see it either. What's going on here?

The reason neither of our mythological students saw the psychic's appearance is that there has never been such a segment of *Oprah*. Sure, Oprah's has done some bizarre shows over the years, but as of this writing, she has yet to sink to such depths as allowing a psychic to come on her program and predict a mass murder on a college campus. And it's a pretty safe bet she never will.

Nevertheless, the feelings of fear on the campuses of the University of San Diego and Bowling Green State University in the fall of 1998 were very palpable. A story published on Oct. 31 in the *San Diego Union-Tribune* said that "most residents [of Camino/Founders Hall] were looking for somewhere else to spend the weekend" due to the spreading of a "classic urban legend." The resident assistants at the dorm said efforts to calm students were largely futile, with one RA saying only four of the 37 women she supervised planned to stay in their dorms Halloween night—"and they've all decided to hang out with me."

The paper quoted one student who spoke with great authority about the danger facing dorm residents: "The psychic predicted that there would be a mass murder at a Southern California school with an H-shaped dorm like ours. They did some research about H-shaped dorms, and only a couple of schools in the nation have them."

On the very same day, more than halfway across the country, a similar story attempting to diffuse the legend appeared in the *Columbus* (Ohio) *Dispatch*. In this version, the killer was supposedly going to be dressed like a clown—an evil killer clown. A veteran official at the university said the story was so familiar to longtime employees that "we may even have a file on this one." Some students had heard the killer would be wearing a Little Bo Peep costume.

Meanwhile, similar rumors about the psychic circulated through the University of Michigan, Kent State University, the

University of Iowa, and the University of Illinois. Patient spokespeople for Oprah's show explained again and again that nothing even remotely resembling such an incident had ever happened. (According to another rumor, the show never aired, but the prediction had occurred. Oprah supposedly told her studio audience she'd never let the segment see the light of day, but word leaked anyway.)

Students at San Diego, Bowling Green, et al., soon realized the scare was borne of pure fiction, but that certainly won't stop the Class of '04 or later generations from going through the whole thing again. The psychic-on-the-talk show story has been around for years; in fact, it's so old that previous versions had the predictor appearing on shows hosted by Phil Donahue and Johnny Carson, both of whom retired long ago.

**UL FOOTNOTE:** On Nov. 1, 1991, just one day after Halloween, a student at the University of Iowa went berserk and shot up the campus, killing four and injuring two before he turned the gun on himself. Weirdly, though, the University of Iowa was one campus where there had never been widespread repetition of the Halloween Killer rumor.

# *The daughter's letter home*

$O$h, the combination of pride and heartbreak when your daughter goes away to college, a thousand miles from the loving comfort and warm embrace of home life. Remember how it was all tears and hugs when you said goodbye to her in late August? But now it's late October and you haven't talked to her on the phone for several weeks. She promised to write every day, but all you've received are a few quick notes and the occasional e-mail with hardly any details of her life on campus. Can it be that your little girl has changed so much, that she doesn't really need you any more?

Then—what do you find when you log on to the family computer? A message from your dear daughter, and a long one at that! You knew she'd come through. Finally, you get some detailed information about her life as a college freshman. You call out to your wife, who excitedly joins you at the computer as you click on the message and begin to read:

Dear Mom and Dad:

Well, it's been nearly three months since I said goodbye to you and began my collegiate career. Please accept my apologies for not talking to you more on the phone or sending you longer notes. You've been in my thoughts every day, but it's things have been so hectic here.

Okay, here goes. I hope you're sitting down, and I hope that as you read this, you remember how much I love you. You're not going to like what you'll learn, so brace yourselves. All I ask is that you please read this letter all the way to the end before you do or say anything.

Oh God, where do I start? How about some good news? You can hardly notice the scar on my forehead, which is pretty remarkable considering I received 47 stitches after I cracked my head open jumping out of my dorm window when the building caught fire. I spent only a few days in the hospital, and my vision is almost totally restored now, so I feel very lucky. It sure could have been worse!

One of the heroes to emerge from the night of the fire was a local, a gas station attendant, who works near campus and happened to be in the area at the time. He was the one who saw me jump from my dorm window, and he called the fire department and the paramedics. He also visited me every day in the hospital, and when it turned out the dorm was going to have to be closed for extensive repairs, he was kind enough to offer me a place to stay—in the basement of his parents' home. I must tell you, they're wonderful people when they're not drinking. They've already accepted me as their daughter-in-law, even though a wedding date hasn't been set yet. I know this is sudden, but don't worry—you guys will be invited to the wedding, too! Dad, I can't imagine getting married to Bruno without you walking me down the aisle with me wearing Mom's dress—that is, if I can still fit into it and the pregnancy doesn't begin to show.

That's right, I'm with child. I know you guys have always looked forward to the day when you'd become grandparents; well, that day is about seven months away! Congratulations.

I know you will welcome Bruno into the family with open arms. He is a kind and thoughtful person—and though he's not well educated, he's quite ambitious. Even though he's of a different race and religion than ours, I know that your oft-expressed views on tolerance and understanding will carry you through the initial difficulty of accepting a black man into the family. He's a strong and brave man, and I really don't blame him for passing on his infection to me, as he wasn't even aware he had syphilis until we got the blood tests for our impending nuptials. I'm sure you'll welcome him to the table when we come home for fall break. That is, if we can make it home. I had to cash in the ticket you sent me to lend Bruno some money to pay off the interest on his gambling debts. If we can't scrounge up enough money for plane tickets (Bruno says he's got "something big" in the works, so keep your fingers crossed), we can always hitchhike.

Now that I have brought you up to date, I'd like to tell you this, Mom and Dad:

There was no dorm fire. I did not crack open my head. I was not in the hospital. I don't know any gas station attendant named Bruno, I'm not pregnant, I don't have syphilis, and I'm still in possession of the plane ticket you sent me.

However, I am getting a D in sociology and an F in algebra. I just told you the rest of that stuff so you'd be able to put this news in perspective.

This story surfaced in the mid-1960s, not as an e-mail message of course, but as a daughter's letter home from college. You can see it as a kind of commentary on the times, with the supposedly liberal parents shocked that their daughter is getting involved in all sorts of mishaps, with the twist being that the supposed wild child really isn't tuning in or turning on or dropping out, she's just having trouble with a couple of freshman courses. What a relief! Sure puts things in perspective, doesn't it?

If a kid ever did write a letter like that, you'd want to smack her, but you'd also have to admit she was a sharp one who should probably change her major to creative writing.

# Secrets of
## fraternity and sorority rituals

I've heard and read about all sorts of bizarre and secret "Greek" rituals—many of them involving the consumption of copious amounts of alcohol and the slaughtering of a chicken or goat—but it's impossible to get any frat brothers or sorority sisters to divulge the secrets of their snobby little cults.

When I asked a friend who had been in a fraternity about the mystery surrounding these secret rituals, he said, "If you're so interested in learning about these things, why don't you contact the Library of Congress? They've been collecting this stuff for years. It's all on the record."

According to popular lore, the Library of Congress started cataloging these rituals in the 1950s, when Sen. Joseph McCarthy's House Committee on Un-American Activities demanded that all fraternities and sororities turn over their secrets to the government, just to prove they weren't communist sympathizers. The information was collected in a volume that still sits in the Library of Congress, where anyone can peruse it for the asking. In fact, the deepest secrets of every fraternity and sorority in the country—with one exception—are contained in the volume. That one exception is the Lambda Chi Alpha fraternity, of which then-President Harry Truman was a member. Truman gave his personal assurance that there was nothing subversive about Lambda Chi, and thus there was no reason for its secrets to be divulged.

That's the only fraternity to be given such an exemption.

Other than Kappa Alpha, that is. FBI director J. Edgar Hoover was a KA, and he saw to it that his fraternity's secrets were not spilled, either...

...And Tau Kappa Epsilon, popularly known as the "Tekes" They eventually were given an exemption, because Ronald Reagan was a brother with Tau Kappa Epsilon, and when he was elected president one of his first official acts was to get TKE's secrets removed from the books.

Also catching a break was Sigma Chi, of which Barry Goldwater was a member. Goldwater lobbied his old colleague and onetime presidential foe Lyndon Johnson to have Sigma Chi's rituals erased from the Library of Congress's collection, and LBJ was happy to oblige.

In the 1990s, powerful women began to exert their influence to get favored sororities removed from the volume. Geraldine Ferraro, Dianne Feinstein, Hillary Clinton, and Elizabeth Dole took care of their respective sororities.

That's an awful lot of exemptions, isn't it? I wonder how many fraternities and sororities still have their secrets exposed in the LOC record book.

Actually, that number would top out at zero. Not because influential alumni have protected their Greek brothers and sisters, but because no such collection was ever put together in the first place. If you call the LOC and start asking questions about this, it won't be long before you're cut off by some poor soul who has already had to address this issue a thousand times. In fact, this myth is so widespread that the Library of Congress uses a form letter to refute it.

An excerpt:

The Library of Congress receives frequent inquiries concerning college fraternity and sorority publications, particularly those detailing secret initiation rites. The Library's general collections do not include any publications which detail secret initiation rites for specific fraternities. The rumor that a collection of documents detailing specific initiation rites exists at the Library of Congress stems from the belief that such publications were requested either by the House Committee on Un-American Activities or by Sen. Joseph McCarthy's Subcommittee of the Senate Government Operations Committee in the 1950s. We have been unable to identify any information to support this...Unpublished materials from these committees are in the custody of the National Archives and Records Administration and are still sealed. No checklist or indexes exist for these documents.

So all you Greeks out there can rest easy—your secrets are safe.

# *Exam scams*

$A$t Urban Legend University, there's a constant battle going on between lazy but clever students who are trying to scam their way through exams by any means necessary, and savvy world-wise professors who attempt to thwart these students with some creative solutions of their own. Each of the following stories is so delicious you'll wish they were true—and, as always, it's impossible to make the claim that none of these incidents *ever* took place.

There's certainly no shortage of students and alumni who will swear one or more of these episodes have occurred at their school, whether that school is Ohio State, Yale, North Carolina, USC, Texas A&M, Grambling, Brown, Case Western, or Slippery Rock. Amazing how such incredible tales are seemingly cloned through the years.

## The stolen exam

There's a scene in *Animal House* where the underachieving Delta boys purloin the carbon of a final exam from a garbage can. Only problem is, the dreaded Omegas are onto the game, and they've switched the real final for a phony version, leaving the Deltas hopelessly unprepared for the big test.

That was the one and only moral lesson in *Animal House*, thank God.

In the urban legend of the stolen exam, it's the teacher who puts a roadblock in the thieving student's attempt to cheat his way to glory. On the day before the test, the student meets with professor, who tells him he needs to get an "A" on the final, or he'll fail the course. The student starts to make his case for leniency, but the professor is called away from the office for a moment. Filled with anxiety, the student paces around the room and pokes around—and that's when he comes across a stack of tests. The final exams, just sitting out in the open! He quickly snatches one copy and jams it into his coat, just before the professor returns to the office.

"Now where were we?" says the professor.

"I was just leaving," the student replies. "Gotta study for the big test!"

His instructor is confused. Why did the kid's mood change so quickly? If this one thinks one night of studying hard is going to adequately prepare him for an exam, let him dream.

The next morning, the instructor counts the tests and realizes one is missing. He had at least a dozen students visit him the day before, and there's no way of knowing which one had the gall to steal a copy of the test—or is there?

Chuckling to himself, the professor takes out a pair of scissors and carefully slices a half-inch from the bottom of each remaining copy of the test. When the students turn in their papers at the end of test, only one literally sticks out—the stolen exam.

Even though the student scored a 96 on the test, he was flunked by the professor, and he didn't utter a peep of protest about it.

## The open-book exam

The instructor of a particularly difficult class in Freshman English tells her students she's going to cut them a big break for the final: it's going to be "open-book." As a matter of fact, she says, students may use "anything you can carry into the classroom" to help them with the test.

Nearly everybody in the class takes this to mean they can come in with books, reference guides, handwritten notes, etc. But one smart-ass freshman football player takes the professor's words literally. After all, she's the one who always says you must choose your words carefully—and she did say "anything you can carry," didn't she? So on the day of the exam, he shows up carrying a nerdy little graduate student under his arm.

"And just what do you think you're doing?" says the professor over the titters of the class.

"You said we could use anything we could carry into the classroom," replies the student. "I'm carrying Dilbert, and he'll be taking the test for me."

Trapped by her own words, the professor has no choice but to allow the graduate student to take the exam for the football player, who winds up with an "A" for the course.

## The stack of blue book exams

This happened in one of those big, impersonal classes you have to take your freshman year, with about 300 other people all packed into some gigantic lecture hall where the teacher has to use a microphone and an overhead projector just to communicate with everyone.

For the final exam, the teacher handed out blue books to the students and told them they had exactly two hours to answer as many of the 200 multiple choice questions as possible. He set a timer to go off in 120 minutes and said that when the buzzer went off, everyone had to stop writing immediately, with no exceptions. Violate this rule and you'd receive an automatic "F."

Two hours later, the alarm sounded, and the professor commanded everyone to drop their pencils and drop off their blue books on the way out. Everyone began filing out—except one frantic kid who kept scribbling away, desperately trying to pencil in a few more answers even though time had expired.

"You there!" the teacher called out. "If you don't stop writing immediately, you're going to be flunked!"

"I just need a minute more, just one minute!" the student pleaded as he continued to write in the blue book.

At that point, it really didn't matter what he said; by this time, the teacher had already doomed the kid to an automatic "F." Most of the class had already turned in their exams, by the time the troublemaker finally gathered his things and clomped down the stairs.

"You might as well keep that exam as a souvenir, because you've already failed this course," said the instructor.

"You've got to be kidding me!" the student cried. "I was only one minute late. What difference does it make?"

The teacher was unmoved. "Rules are rules. If I let you have an extra minute I'd have to let everyone have an extra minute, wouldn't I?"

"Do you know who I am?" said the student. "Do you know what my *name* is?"

"No I don't, and I couldn't care less," replied the teacher.

"Good!" said the student—and with that he jammed his blue book right in the middle of the stack before dashing out of there.

I've included this story because I've heard it at least 20 times over the last decade, but to me, there's a gaping flaw in the telling. Okay, the teacher doesn't know the names of all the students in the overcrowded class, so he wouldn't be able to identify the student by name as he's grading the tests. But once he was finished with the grading process, couldn't he require all students to show up, with student ID's, to claim their exams? All he'd have to do is make a face identification of the culprit, hang on to that particular exam and change the grade to an "F."

Most urban legends, even the ones that defy logic, have a nice little airtight quality about them; that's why they survive through myriad retellings. This one should fade—not because it's implausible, but because of the obvious way in which the teacher could have nailed the student, thus negating the twist.

## The letter home to mom

Once again, the ubiquitous blue book plays a part in an exam scam classic.

Our unprepared student freaks out when he's confronted with a complicated essay question that will count for 100 percent of the test. He has no idea what to say—this is the one portion of the textbook he didn't study! To make matters worse, the professor has given each student *two* blue books, indicating that he expects a long and detailed answer.

And then a light bulb goes off. The student starts writing in a blue book—but he's not answering the question, he's writing a letter to his mother. "I really think I did well on the essay," he writes. "I finished ahead of everyone else in the class so I figured I'd write to you, dear mother. I don't want to get up and leave early—it'll seem like I'm showing off. Anyway, let me tell you about this class. I'm so lucky to have had this teacher! He's by far the smartest and most inspirational teacher I've ever had..."

At the end of the class, the student turns in the letter to mom and then runs back to his dorm room, where he opens the textbook for the class and uses it as a reference guide as he composes a thoughtful and comprehensive answer to the essay question. He then mails that blue book to his mother in Boston.

That night the professor rings the student and says, "I don't know how to tell you this, but we have a big problem."

"You're kidding me," says the student. "To be honest with you, I thought I aced the test."

"You very well might have, for all I know," says the teacher. "I haven't seen your answers."

"I don't understand."

"I've got a letter to your mother here instead of your essay. Does that make any sense to you?"

"Oh no!" says the student, trying his best to sound shocked. "That means I must have mailed the test to my mom. This is the most embarrassing thing that's ever happened to me."

The student says he'll call his mother right away and instruct her to send the envelope straight to the professor; that way, the teacher will know the story is legitimate. Sure enough, an envelope arrives at the professor's office a few days later, and he opens it to find the student's test, which of course contains a beautifully written essay. Not only does the professor give the kid an "A," he sends the other booklet to the student's mother with a note attached telling her what a pleasure it was having the lad in his class.

## The flat tire excuse

Three smart (and incredibly cocky) fraternity brothers were so confident they'd ace their chemistry final that they went on a weekend road trip before the exam, which was scheduled for Monday at 10 a.m. They spent all weekend partying with some girls from a nearby school and never once even bothered to pick up a book, even though the final was going to count for 50 percent of their grade.

Problem was, they overslept Monday morning. By the time they made it back to campus it was noon, and they knew the professor would be busy collecting exam booklets from the other students. Suddenly the "As" or "Bs" they counted on receiving for the class were looking like "Ds" at best! Depression set in. What to do?

"I've got the plan!" said one of the brothers as they crossed the quad and headed for the classroom. "We'll tell the professor we were doing a charity thing—like a dance marathon—and we overslept this morning because we were so tired from dancing, and as we were racing back to campus, we got a flat tire and it took forever to get the thing fixed."

The three charmers told the story to their stupid professor, who fell for it hook, line, and sinker.

"All right boys, I'm not going to penalize you for your good intentions, even though you should have given yourself more time to return to campus," he said. "I'll see you here bright and early tomorrow morning. You'll have two hours to take the exam." The frat boys exchanged knowing glances on the way out the door. Any teacher who falls for that deserves to get taken for a ride. The boys spent the rest of the day studying to reassure themselves, and their cocky swagger had returned by the next morning, when they entered the otherwise empty classroom.

"There's nobody in either of the adjoining classrooms, so each of you gets your own room," said the professor. "Not that I'd accuse you boys of cheating or anything, but we'll play it on the safe side."

These guys didn't care, as they weren't *cheaters* or anything; they were just resourceful types who had figured out a way to buy a little time from their unsophisticated instructor.

In the separate classrooms, each young man tackled the exam. The first question was worth five points, and it's a breeze. At about the same time, each of the boys flipped to the second page, where they found this message:

"Question #2 (worth 95 points): Which tire?"

The cries of anguish could be heard through the building. Of course, the boys never discussed which tire supposedly went flat.

# *Porn 'n' Chicken*

An Ivy League porn film!

It's the ultimate in high concept filmmaking—and it's a four-word description the media can't resist. For more than a year now, reporters have been salivating and snickering about a group of Yale students who said they planned to write, produce, direct, and yes, star in a porno flick called "The StaXXX."

First the *Yale Daily News* reported the story, then the *New York Times* picked it up—and after that the media hunt was on. *The New Yorker*, *The London Evening Standard*, *The Boston Globe*, *Premiere* magazine, numerous TV stations, *Hustler*, *Time*, even Danish Public Radio for crying out loud—all weighed in with the salacious details of the shocking production.

From the Evening Standard:

> Work has already begun on "The StaXXX," a feature film based on the sexual rituals of one of the 300-year-old university's secret societies, with assurances given to students who volunteer to act that their identities will be concealed in order to spare them the embarrassment in their future careers as politicians, lawyers, and other pillars of the establishment.

Quoting one of the anonymous filmmakers, the *Standard* reported: "The film's 'action sequences' will be improvised by the actors and reportedly include 'heterosexual and homosexual sequences, as well as scenes exploring fetishism, group sex, and nonphysical intercourse. Highly identifiable Yale locations [will be used], including the Sterling Memorial Library Stacks."

Hence the title "The StaXXX," playing off the library locale, as well as the "tradition" of porn movies and starlets using triple-X as a way of indicating they're *really* naughty, e.g., "Nikki SeXXX starring in 'EXXXSTASY on a XXXYLOPHONE,' rated XXX!"

As the story gained momentum in the press in the fall and winter of 2000-2001, the filmmakers, who go by pseudonyms such as "Baby Gristle" and "Canadian Bacon," claimed they were going to premiere the movie in conjunction with the university's 300-year anniversary celebration in April, which was to be attended by President George W. Bush, class of '68, and his Poppy, class of '48. (The screening never happened.) They also claimed that one scene, involving two female students in an explicit encounter, already had been filmed—but the footage was destroyed after one of the producers drunkenly revealed the name of one of the women at a party, which led to a reporter calling her father, which led to her father going ballistic, which led to the "actress" demanding that the tape be destroyed.

Other media reports said the movie had its genesis in a secret society known as Porn 'n' Chicken, which consists of a bunch of students getting together to, well, eat take-out chicken and watch dirty movies. (When I was in college we did the same thing, but we called it, "Going to college.") Writers from *Premiere* and *Time* sat in with the group in separate sessions and wrote cheeky pieces about their adventures—but neither reporter saw any footage shot by the Yale students. They just sat around with a bunch of smart and smart-alecky kids, watching porn and meeting their greasy-food maximum for the week in one sitting.

Sniff sniff sniff. That scent you're picking up isn't fried chicken; it's the whiff of an elaborate hoax. Porn 'n' Chicken is most likely just a cover name for the Pundits, a semi-legendary group of clever pranksters at Yale. As of this writing, the *Porn 'n' Chicken* gang was still sticking to their story, and they were maintaining that at least three major agencies in Hollywood were interested in representing the rights—not to "The StaXXX," but to the story *about* the movie.

I ain't buying it.

I'm not saying that I'm not going to purchase the film when it becomes available. I'm saying I'm not buying this story.

The producers said "The StaXXX" will be shot in "Eyes Wide Shut" style, with the performers' faces obscured by masks or camera angles, so as not to jeopardize the senatorial or big business ambitions of the participants. Right. As if the names wouldn't leak like the Titanic, post-iceberg. Just ask the young woman whose name was blurted out in the first place—if such a scene was shot in the first place, that is.

To what end are these students making this movie? If it's for public consumption, the moment they put it out there in any fashion—signing release statements and contracts and providing birth dates and Social Security numbers in order to be paid royalties and file tax returns—is the moment the names will start tumbling out of Yale like dice from a Yahtzee cup. Anyone who thinks they can participate in a sensational movie like this and retain anonymity would be too naïve and stupid to gain entrance into Yale in the first place. As the actor calling himself Canadian Bacon wrote in an e-mail to the Boston Globe, "If I become a senator and you have me on your database somehow as being involved in this film, that makes a pretty good story, right?"

Um, yes. So why are you perching on that limb already, Bacon boy?

In March 2000, the putative makers of "The StaXXX" agreed to take my e-mailed questions about the project, and added that they'd love for me to review it on *Ebert & Roeper and the Movies* once it's released. (For the record: we don't review porn films on the show. We do, however, review Tom Green movies, which might be worse.) I quickly dispatched a number of questions about their so-called film in an attempt to pin down details that would either confirm its existence or reveal the whole thing to be a prank. I also asked point-blank: "Is this a hoax?"

Weeks passed. I wrote a column about the movie, questioning its veracity. A few days later, Baby Gristle of "the board of governors of Porn 'n' Chicken" e-mailed an apology for not answering my questions and added, "If things haven't soured between us, we'd like to keep you updated about the release of the film."

OK, I'll hold my breath, starting…never.

Actually, things haven't soured between us at all; in fact, I admire the Porn 'n' Chicken gang for their innovation and their dogged determination and most of all for their ability to keep a collective straight face during this prolonged ruse. If you can get everyone from the *New York Times* to Danish Public Radio to gobble your story, I'd say you've pulled one for the ages. But if these smarty-pants Yalies ever get around to actually filming and releasing "The StaXXX," they can say goodbye to the "Baby Gristle" and "Canadian Bacon" pseudonyms and say hello to their new lives as the people who will forever be tagged as the Ivy League Porno Gang.

And won't that look good on the resume?

**UL FOOTNOTE:** In 2000, Freddie Prinze Jr. and Julia Stiles starred in "Down to You," a fluffy romantic comedy about students at an elite Eastern college. A subplot involved a group of students who filmed and starred in their own porn movies. Hmmmmmm.

Chapter Three

# LEGENDS OF THE SILVER SCREEN

In the summer of 1998, I interviewed Mickey Rooney, who told me a story about his days as a child prodigy. "When I was five years old," he said. "I went to Walt Disney's office for lunch. He was drawing at his desk, and I climbed onto his lap and said, 'Whatcha drawing, Uncle Walt?'"

"He showed me this drawing of a mouse and told me it was for a new cartoon he was working on. He said he was thinking of calling him Marty Mouse, and what did I think of that name?"

"I told him I had a better name—mine. I said, 'Why don't you call him Mickey Mouse, Uncle Walt?' and he said, 'I just might do that.'"

You gotta love Mickey Rooney. For one thing, he was born in 1920, which means he was eight, not five, when Mickey Mouse debuted in the cartoon *Steamboat Willie*. For another, Walt Disney came up with the idea and the name for the mouse while he was taking a train home after learning his first cartoon series, *Alice Comedies*, had been canceled. And there is no record of little Mickey Rooney being on that train.

But it's a harmless tale, and besides, we all know that Hollywood is a make-believe place populated by make-believe people who tell make-believe stories about their make-believe lives. The quotes attributed to stars and studio heads, the tidy anecdotes told through the years about casting decisions and movie-star romances and the creation of classic films—a lot of these juicy tales are spiced heavily with apocryphal details.

Do stories like the one told by Mickey Rooney qualify as urban legends? Well, maybe they're glamorous cousins to the UL...

# *The ghost in*
# *Three Men and a Baby*

A year or so after the release of the surprisingly successful comedy *Three Men and a Baby* on video, a *Sun-Times* reader called to tell me there was something really scary about that movie.

"There's a ghost of a dead little boy in the background of one scene."

"Of course there is," I said, before gently suggesting the caller double the dosage of whatever medication he was taking.

Little did I know the reader was right—sort of.

When *Three Men and a Baby* was released in 1987, nary a word was said about any eerie ghost-boy. But after it was out on video for a while, stories began circulating about a ghostly figure who had made an unscheduled and inexplicable cameo in the otherwise harmless comedy.

The apparition appears in a scene in which Jack Holden (Ted Danson) is visited by his mother (Celeste Holm) in the trendy loft apartment Jack shares with his two bachelor buddies. As Jack's mom cradles the infant in her arms, the chilling image of a little boy appears behind sheer curtains in front of a window in the background, but neither character makes mention of it. Why should they? It's obviously not a part of the story itself.

Nobody on the set saw the boy while the scene was being filmed, but he's clearly visible to anyone who rents the movie.

Only later did the filmmakers learn that a 9-year-old boy committed suicide with a shotgun in the very apartment they had selected as the home for the three men and their baby, and the figure in the background is the ghost of that poor little boy. If you watch closely, you can see the curtains move, revealing a shotgun in the ghost's grip.

The boy's parents had moved out of the trendy apartment after the terrible tragedy but had been unable to sell the place, which explains why such a great locale was available to the movie company at a bargain rate.

When the boy's mother saw *Three Men and a Baby* for the first time on video, she let out a blood-curdling scream as she recognized the image of her son—in his funeral clothes, no less. She tried to get the producers to cut the scene or edit it in some way, but they refused. So she made the talk show rounds, telling Phil Donahue, Oprah Winfrey, and Geraldo Rivera of her anguish and suffering. Unfortunately, even the publicity blitz couldn't ease her pain, and she ended up in a mental institution, where she remains to this day.

Or so the story goes. In reality, the "ghost" is a cardboard cutout of Ted Danson in top hat and tails. (It's not life-size, which is why people thought the "ghost" was a little boy.) His character in the movie, you might recall, was an actor, and the original script called for a running joke about a dog food commercial in which Danson's character appeared in formal wear. That element didn't make it into the final version of the movie, but the cardboard cutout makes a couple of appearances—first near the window, and then later in the movie, when the baby's mother (Nancy Travis) returns to reclaim the baby.

And for the record: the supposedly haunted apartment was created on a soundstage. It is not real.

*Three Men and a Baby* spawned a sequel, *Three Men and a Little Lady*, which didn't do nearly as well as the original, and effectively killed the franchise.

# *The munchkin suicide*

You probably never thought about this, but munchkins are people, too, and they can fall in love just like everyone else. That means they can get their little munchkin hearts broken to the point where they don't want to go on living their little munchkin lives any more. Such was the case with the munchkin actor who was so devastated about being dumped by a female little person that he committed suicide, hanging himself on the set of *The Wizard of Oz*—a death that was inadvertently captured during filming and somehow made its way into the final print of the movie.

I rented a copy of *The Wizard of Oz* and fast-forwarded to the legendary scene where you can supposedly view the munchkin swaying from a tree. We pick up the action as Dorothy (Judy Garland) and the Scarecrow (Ray Bolger) are following the Yellow Brick Road on their way to the Emerald City. They try to pick some fruit but they're rebuffed by talking trees. They meet the Tin Man (Jack Haley), and are confronted by the Wicked Witch of the West (Margaret Hamilton), who tries to torch the Scarecrow.

Stay with the scene to the end, as Dorothy, the Tin Man, and the Scarecrow make their way down the Yellow Brick Road and away from the camera. There in the trees is some sort of movement—perhaps the eerie form of a sad munchkin, hanging himself.

Other rumors said it wasn't a suicide, it was just a hapless stagehand who had taken a tumble from the rafters. In either case, there's no doubt something is occurring in those trees. Nobody noticed it when the movie was released in 1939 or during any of the subsequent theatrical re-issues over the years—but when a special-edition, 50th anniversary video was issued in 1989, *Oz* buffs noticed the rustling in the trees, and an urban legend was born. (That Judy Garland would often appear on talk shows in the 1950s and 1960s, telling greatly exaggerated tales of munchkin shenanigans probably added some credibility to the notion of a munchkin suicide caught on film.)

So what exactly are we seeing in that scene? According to a number of *Oz* experts, including the narrator on *The Ultimate Oz* laser disc, it's a bird. The scene in question was shot on a soundstage. In order to make the set look more "real," the filmmakers used a number of exotic birds, including peacocks, emus, and cranes. As Dorothy, the Tin Man, and the Scarecrow head away from the camera, a large bird rustles in the trees and spreads its wings.

Stephen Cox, author of *The Munchkins of Oz* (1996), advanced this explanation in a 1997 column by Cecil "The Straight Dope" Adams. Cox told Adams he'd heard the suicide theory, but what we're seeing is a large bird—"maybe a crane or stork," writes Adams. Whatever make and model of bird we're looking at, it's nothing more than a slight distraction, and since director Victor Fleming wanted birds in the scene in the first place, there was no reason to shoot another take.

In a 1996 interview with the *Orlando Sentinel*, then-81-year-old Meinhardt Raabe, who played the coroner of Munchkin Land (the man who had the qualifications to say if a witch was "not only merely dead, but really most sincerely dead") said he'd never heard the hanging munchkin rumor until about 1993, but of course it wasn't true: "They put an Australian emu in the background...it's crazy, like watching clouds in the sky. People see all sorts of things in Oz."

# *Back to the Future II predicts the World Series*

The original *Back to the Future*, with Michael J. Fox as time-traveling high school student Marty McFly, was a clever and entertaining romp that deserved its critical and commercial kudos. Fox and the rest of the cast were uniformly excellent, the script and direction were sharp and lively, and the tunes from Huey Lewis and the News were perfect for the mood of the film. They should have left well enough alone, but of course they didn't. Alas, *Back to the Future II* and the imaginatively titled *Back to the Future III* were jumbled, garish, convoluted, and just plain stupid.

There is, however, one redeeming element to *BTTF II* and that is the contribution of a pretty decent urban legend to the popular culture. According to movie buff lore, the 1989 movie correctly forecasts the 1997 Word Series triumph of the Florida Marlins—a prediction made even more astounding when you consider that the Marlins didn't even exist in 1989!

However, it's only about 10 percent true. The movie picks up where the first "Back to the Future" ends, with Christopher Lloyd's Doc Brown telling Marty there's a problem with his kids. Wandering around in the year 2015, Marty sees a holographic sports broadcast announcing that the Chicago Cubs have won the World Series by defeating "Miami." (No nickname is given for the team.) He's distracted by this announcement as an old man approaches and asks him for a donation to save the clock tower.

The joke is that the woeful Cubs finally win the World Series, and the mentioning of Miami being in the Series was a nod to the inevitable expansion that would have taken place by 2015. There was no Miami team in the major leagues in the late 1980s, but it would be a pretty safe bet that such a large metropolis would have its own club by then.

There was no reason for this episode to spawn an urban legend when the movie came out, but when the Florida Marlins shocked the world by upsetting the Cleveland Indians in the 1997 World Series, some movie fans with inaccurate memories of *BTTF II* started talking about how the movie actually foresaw the Marlins' miracle season. Some versions of the rumor had either Marty or his rival Biff saying something like, "That'll be the day" when they hear the announcement of the World Series victory.

None of this happens in the film. It's the Cubs, not the unnamed Miami team, who are named as the World Series champs—and besides, the broadcast in the movie has to do with the 2015 season. Why would a program on the air in 2015 be announcing the results of the 1997 Series?

# *The Marisa Tomei Oscar mistake*

It's hard to make the case that Marisa Tomei's performance as the long-suffering girlfriend of Joe Pesci in the 1992 comedy *My Cousin Vinny* was worthy of an Academy Award. She was adorable, all right, and she had the Brooklyn accent down cold, but come on. If Marisa's work was Oscar-worthy, why did the Academy snub Ralph Macchio from the same movie for Best Supporting Actor?

Even after Tomei was nominated, she was considered a longshot. The Supporting Actress field was loaded that year with esteemed actors in prestige projects: Miranda Richardson in *Damage*, Joan Plowright in *Enchanted April*, Vanessa Redgrave in *Howard's End*, and Judy Davis in *Husbands and Wives*. Take a look at that list and you can see few people were picking Marisa Tomei from *My Cousin Vinny*!

Traditionally at the Academy Awards, the previous year's winner in a similar category announces the nominees and the winner, so for the 1993 ceremony, the presenter for Best Supporting Actress was Jack Palance, who had won the Best Supporting Actor trophy the previous year for *City Slickers*. Palance stumbled a bit as he read the names of the nominees; then he tore open the envelope and said, "And the Oscar goes to...Marisa Tomei for *My Cousin Vinny*."

A ripple of surprise ran through the audience, with Tomei looking more surprised than anyone. She was probably thinking to herself, *There must be some kind of mistake.*

She wouldn't be the only one entertaining such a thought. The curtain had barely dropped on the 1993 Academy Awards ceremony when the rumors began circulating about Tomei's shocking victory. According to the story, the elderly Palance—who did seem a bit shaky and lost during his appearance—had a made a horrible mistake when it was time to read the winner. Instead of calling out Vanessa Redgrave's name, he became confused and read Tomei's name because alphabetically she was the last of the five nominees, and her name was still on the teleprompter. Before he could correct his error, the music had swelled up, Tomei had popped out of her seat and the audience members had recovered from their surprise and were giving the startled young actress a hearty round of applause. The confused Palance never had a chance to say another word, and officials from the Academy decided to cover up the whole thing, rather than risk their credibility by admitting the gaffe. Some say Tomei was informed backstage of the mix-up but refused to part with her trophy; others claim she's still in the dark, although she's no doubt heard the rumors by now.

This rumor became so widespread by 1994 that the *Hollywood Reporter* did a story about the supposed foul-up, making the claim that it was being circulated by the "former son-in-law of a distinguished Academy Award winner." Huh? Why would the *former* son-in-law of some old Oscar winner want to spread such a tale? What would be the upside for him? And how would he know anyway?

A few years later, a famous film critic made a few television appearances in which he claimed the Tomei story was true, and that there was a massive cover-up in Hollywood to keep the public in the dark. Of course, he offered no proof of any such conspiracy.

The Orange County, California *Register* attempted to kill the story in a 1994 article, "For Outstanding Achievement in the Art of Oscar Rumors," and my colleague at the *Sun-Times*, Roger Ebert, also tried to douse it in a 1997 feature. Nevertheless, there are those who believe to this day that Marisa Tomei should scratch her name off that Academy Award and hand it over to Ms. Redgrave.

Here's the official explanation from the Motion Picture Academy. At every Academy Awards ceremony since 1953, two accountants from the firm of Price Waterhouse are stationed in the wings for the duration of the ceremony. These individuals know the names of all the winners well beforehand; in fact, they are the only two people who have this knowledge in advance. They have standing instructions to immediately go onstage and make a correction if the wrong name is read for any reason.

To date, that has never happened. Marisa Tomei won the 1992 Academy Award fair and square, and no amount of petty squabbling, irresponsible rumor-mongering, or jealous back-biting can take that away from her.

# The Twister tornado

Boy those people in *Twister* were idiots. Every time they got wind (so to speak) of a big tornado, they'd pack up their whiz-bang scientific equipment, hop into their pickup trucks and chase right after the storm, all the while whooping it up and cranking the stereo as if they were on the way to Spring Break or something. These weren't ordinary tornadoes, either; these were monster tornadoes that could fling cows around, tornadoes that actually made ominous groaning noises that sounded like the shark's soundtrack in *Jaws*. How does a wispy Helen Hunt stand a chance against something like that?

Even though the so-called plot of *Twister* was about as complicated as a *game* of Twister, I have to admit the movie was wildly entertaining, due mostly to the incredible special effects that made you feel as if the characters were facing off against real tornadoes and not blank screens and computer-generated effects. If you saw the movie in a theater with a top quality screen and sound system, you were practically pinned in your seats by the action—and if you happened to catch *Twister* on a certain night at a particular drive-in located in southern Ontario, Canada, you really thought the special effects were amazing, especially when the tornado appeared to blast right through the screen.

In an incredible twist(er) of fate, the movie was playing at a drive-in theater just outside Thorgold, Ontario, when a real tornado tore through the area, causing extensive property damage.

Incredibly, the tornado's path cut right through the drive-in screen during one of the tornado sequences in the movie, creating the most realistic 3-D effect in the history of cinema. No one at the theater was injured by the blast, but the screen was destroyed. Patrons were offered refunds, but many of them said they didn't want their money back, as they'd never been so entertained in their lives.

The *London Daily Telegraph* was among the newspapers reporting this story. In a May 24, 1996 column, Mark Steyn wrote about one of the patrons who was at the drive-in theater when the tornado supposedly struck: "During one of the duller passages [in the movie], one guy went to the bathroom, and came back to find the screen vibrating wildly and a loud whooshing filling the air. Pleasantly surprised to find that for once the computerized effects and Surround sound were all they were cracked up to be, he took a moment to realize it was a real twister. Seconds later, the screen was ripped out of the ground and came crashing down on top of the cars, sending the crowd fleeing for their lives. I'd like to think God was reminding the audience that He is the ultimate special effect..."

That must have been one incredibly stupid man, to think even for a split second that he was witnessing the ultimate in special effects and not *standing in the middle of a tornado!*

Let's set the urban legend aside and review the facts. It is true that on May 20, 1996, a tornado struck the town of Thorgold—and the screen at a drive-in theater called the Can-View 4 did sustain damage. And sure enough, the movie *Twister* was scheduled to play on that particular screen. However, the tornado struck during the light of day, and we all know drive-in movies don't open until after dark.

# *Legends of Titanic*

It's hard to believe now, but before *Titanic* became a billion-dollar triumph at the box office and a huge success at the Academy Awards, there were grave doubts about the commercial viability of the movie. Not wanting to take a financial bath all by itself, Paramount ended up sharing the frighteningly high production costs with Twentieth Century Fox, and Cameron even forfeited his director's fee so a few million more could be poured into the budget. In the fall of 1997, with *Titanic* set to launch in December of that year, advance buzz on the movie was mixed at best.

So there was much concern when Cameron's first cut came in with a running time of nearly four hours. Even with some last-minute trims, *Titanic* had a daunting length of three hours, 14 minutes. Not only would this limit the number of times the film could be shown in a day, but there was great concern that audiences wouldn't want to sit in a theater that long, regardless of how strong the reviews might be.

In a *Los Angeles Times* story published in December of 1997, about three weeks before the film was to be released, an executive on the film was asked about the last-minute cuts Cameron had made. "The movie went from three hours, 36 minutes, to two hours, 74 minutes," said the exec.

From that joking response, an urban myth was launched. Soon the gossip world was buzzing with stories that theater owners—who are usually leery of any movies that run for more than three hours—had been duped into thinking "Titanic' wasn't three hours long because it was being promoted as having an official time of "two hours, 74 minutes."

Check out this *Good Morning America* transcript from Dec. 31, 1997, as reviewer Joel Siegel jokingly discusses the issue with anchor Tom Bergeron:

SIEGEL:        Three hours go by in a minute, and it's doing incredible business. This Friday, it'll hit $100 million, considering they only get one show a night.

BERGERON:   That's right.

SIEGEL:        Now, it's bad luck to have a three-hour movie, so they're advertising it as two hours and 74 minutes long.

Two weeks later, on Jan. 15, 1998, Siegel revisited the topic with Charles Gibson and Nancy Snyderman.

SIEGEL:        [*Titanic* has] grossed over $200 million. It's amazing, because it's the first movie ever, I think, to gross more than $20 million four weekends in a row.

GIBSON:        Wow.

SNYDERMAN: Oh, that's interesting, a new stat.

SIEGEL:        A new stat. And it's long. They only get one showing a night.

SNYDERMAN: Yes.

SIEGEL:        Because the movie—

SNYDERMAN: It's three hours plus.

| SIEGEL: | Three hours and 14 minutes. Although it's supposed to be the kiss of death in Hollywood, they have a movie over three hours, so they're advertising it as two hours and 74 minutes long—which is actually longer than it took the ship to sink. It took the ship two hours and 40 minutes to sink; it takes you two hours and 74 minutes to see the movie. |
|---|---|

Siegel was obviously having fun with the story, but his comments only served to fuel the silly fire.

It's a bit of a misconception that it's bad luck for a movie to run more than three hours. Obviously that didn't hold true for *Titanic*, nor did three-hour-plus running times hurt *Schindler's List*, *Dances With Wolves* or *Braveheart*, all huge commercial successes and Academy Award winners for Best Picture. As for theater owners, they probably would prefer movies to run less than two hours—that way you get more customers in your lobby to buy popcorn—but you still have more than one showing per night if a film runs three hours. Theaters were showing *Titanic* at 3:30 p.m., 7 p.m., and 10:30 p.m., for example. And in this age of multi-screen megaplexes, viewers had the opportunity to see the movie practically every hour.

Nevertheless, the story that Paramount was "advertising" the running length at two hours and 74 minutes continued to grow. There was even a bogus posting on the Internet of a London newspaper story saying that some Brits were offended by the American studio's attempt to fool them into thinking the movie wasn't all that long.

The newspaper article doesn't exist—because the studio never tried to pull such a stunt, overseas or anywhere else. Greg Brilliant, vice-president of national publicity for Paramount, said, "Paramount never had another running time for *Titanic*.

We never officially promoted it that way. It was an inside running joke in Hollywood, but there was never a statement issued or anything."

Besides, studios almost never list the running time of a movie in their advertising materials; check your local paper's movie section and you'll see what I mean. It's true that many film reviewers include the movie's length in the credit boxes that run with the text, but in those cases the running time is almost always listed in pure minutes. So in the case of *Titanic*, the length was listed at 194 minutes.

Does Arnold Schwarzenegger make a cameo appearance in *Titanic*? That was the rumor going around when the movie was released on video. Supposedly Cameron had completely run out of money, but he needed a few shots for the ballroom sequence, so he spliced in a few quick cuts from the opening of *True Lies*, in which secret agent Arnold spins around the dance floor of a black-tie ball with Tia Carrera.

Doubtful. For one thing, the costumes wouldn't have matched, what with *Titanic* taking place more than 80 years ago, and *True Lies* set in modern times. Besides, Arnold Schwarzenegger is four times the size of Leonardo DiCaprio, and he would have stuck out like a linebacker at a pee-wee football game.

## *Disney's secret messages*

For years, the Walt Disney Co. denied or simply ignored all rumors and reports about subliminal messages or naughty images cropping up in their wildly popular and wholesome full-length feature cartoons.

Until *The Rescuers* controversy. This R-rated moment Disney had to acknowledge, because it wasn't an urban myth, it was undisputedly real.

You had to go about 38 minutes into a tainted copy of *The Rescuers* to catch a glimpse of the little picture that, in January of 1999, prompted Disney to recall more than 3.4 million copies of the 1977 animated feature.

In the offending scene, a couple of mice named Bernard and Bianca are flying through town in a small box strapped to the back of an albatross. When they pass by a particular building, a topless woman can be glimpsed through a window. It's not visible at normal speed, as the image appears on just two of the movie's 110,000-plus frames. You have to hit the pause button on the VCR and do a frame-by-frame advance. Eventually, you will clearly see the naked torso of a grownup gal. Then it disappears for a moment before showing up again, in the same window.

It's not exactly a shocking image, even for a Disney cartoon. Heck, some observers noted that the title character in *Pocahantas* looked, moved and talked like Christy Turlington, and Esmerelda's pole-dance in *The Hunchback of Notre Dame* was nearly as provocative as Elizabeth Berkley's gyrations in *Showgirls*—and those were intentional images.

The images in *The Rescuers*, however, left no room for interpretation. You couldn't claim people were really looking at a window plant or a lamp or a pillow—it was a topless woman, no doubt about it. The honchos at Disney had little choice but to recall the movie, which was issued on video in December 1998 after theatrical showings in 1977, 1983 and 1989. ("The Rescuers" was first released on video in 1992, but a Disney spokesman said those copies were made from a different print, which didn't contain the topless woman's cameo.) Supposedly, the handiwork was not the product of some mischievous animator, but someone messing around during post-production.

"This was something that was done more than 20 years ago," said a Disney spokesman, who categorized the controversy as "an internal matter." And a particularly embarrassing and exasperating situation for Disney, what with all those rumors in the past about subliminal images in films.

Let's take a look at some of the more enduring stories, and whether the claims about them have any veracity:

In *The Little Mermaid*, there was a widespread report that in the first wedding scene (where a disguised Ursula tries to wed Prince Eric), the minister becomes visibly aroused. After taking another look at this sequence, I'd have to say this one is total bunk. The minister is kneeling; those are his *knees* sticking out from under his tunic. You'd have to be a sex-obsessed, insanely repressed bluenose to see anything else. I guess that explains why some ultra-conservative groups bleated long and loud about it.

Less clear-cut was the supposedly suggestive message appearing in *The Lion King*. Lore has it that the letters S-E-X appear in a cloud of dust at one point, but again, you see what you want to see. It does seem as if three letters are formed in the sky, but to me it looks more like S-F-X, which is movie-speak for "special effects." Maybe an animator was having a little fun putting in a plug for the technical wizards.

Either that or it's just a cloud of dust.

Then there's the claim that in *Aladdin* the title character blurts, "All good teenagers take off their clothes!"

Here we're getting into grassy knoll territory. At some point you have to ask *why* the incredibly successful Disney empire would risk its status as the Unofficial Sponsor of America's Childhood by inserting stupidly suggestive words or images in movies destined to earn hundreds of millions of dollars in profits. For that matter, why would some Disney employee risk a successful career with a great company on a silly little practical joke?

Apparently these thoughts didn't occur to *Movie Guide* magazine, a Christian entertainment publication, which in 1995 ran a story about the "take off your clothes" line and drew comparisons to the heavy metal bands of old that supposedly "backmasked" Satanic messages into their albums. According to an article in the *Wall Street Journal* that detailed the controversy, the magazine exhorted "moral Americans" to contact Disney chairman Michael Eisner and ask him to remove the "manipulative subliminal messages" from its movies. The article prompted conservative groups such as the American Life League to protest, which led to an *Associated Press* article on the controversy, which meant dozens of mainstream newspapers picked up on it. Nobody seemed to notice or care when the publisher of *Movie Guide* finally got around to viewing *Aladdin* and quickly printed a retraction because he realized Disney was telling the truth.

*Freeze-frame alert*: According to the book *Mouse Under Glass* by David Koenig, *Aladdin* supposedly also contains more "traditional" hidden treats. For example, in a scene where Jafar enters a room and a stack of toys collapses, one of the toys is the Beast from *Beauty and the Beast*. And, at the end of the movie, when Rajah grows from a cub to a tiger, he sprouts a Mickey Mouse head for a split second.

*The Rescuers* doesn't mark the first time a fleeting surprise has appeared in a Disney film. The theatrical, early videocassette, and laserdisc versions of *Who Framed Roger Rabbit* (which is not a children's movie) reportedly contained a number of racy images, including Baby Huey extending his middle finger, a mini-skirted and pantyless Jessica Rabbit briefly flashing the audience, and graffiti on a men's room wall stating, "For a Good Time Call Allyson Wonderland." In the climactic scene, Winnie the Pooh's sidekick, Piglet, was glimpsed hanging off a caboose—and in every window in that train there's a violent act taking place. However, those alleged pranks do not appear in the video of *Who Framed Roger Rabbit* that I watched in early 1999.

More benign—but definitely there for the spotting—are the quick cameos in *The Hunchback of Notre Dame*. According to Disneyphiles, if you freeze-frame your way through the second musical number, you'll spot Belle from *The Beauty and the Beast*, Pumbaa from *The Lion King,* and a merchant who has the flying carpet from *Aladdin*. (There's also what appears to be a satellite dish on one roof.)

Given recent controversy over *The Rescuers*, something tells me the current crop of Disney animators, digitizers, and other technical pros will think twice before inserting any unsanctioned tricks into movies. You just wouldn't want to face the wrath of Mickey!

# *Snuff said*

In an early scene from Joel Schumacher's ludicrously over-wrought and yet highly entertaining 1999 shock-o-drama, *8mm*, private investigator Nicolas Cage is summoned to the mansion of a little old lady in a wheelchair whose billionaire business-man husband has just passed away. As the old gal's lawyer explains, the geezer left more than stocks and bonds in his personal safe; there was also a single canister of film, containing searing images of a young girl seemingly being murdered. When the lawyer asks Cage if he knows about the existence of such hideously evil movies, Cage explains that snuff films are "kind of an urban myth."

Except in this movie, of course. *8mm* takes us on a grisly rollercoaster ride as Cage sinks deep into the mire of the underground porn scene, where leather-clad weirdos in cave-like structures hawk sick movies. After following a number of dead-end trails and false leads, Cage discovers snuff films really do exist, courtesy of an infamous filmmaker from New York. We now realize the girl Cage has been hired to find really was murdered on film.

The release of *8mm* sparked renewed debate about whether snuff films exist in the real world. Clarification: we're not talking about murders, suicides, or fatal accidents that have been caught on film or tape, as in the infamous *Faces of Death* shockumentaries (which combine staged scenes with footage of real autopsies and accidents), or the videotape of Pennsylvania public official R. Budd Dwyer shooting himself at a press conference; or *Execution*, a popular video showing the government-mandated deaths of nearly two dozen people in separate incidents. In a "real" snuff movie, the victim thinks she's appearing in a low-budget thriller or porno movie, but soon realizes the filmmakers aren't going to pretend to kill her, they're going to end her life as the camera rolls. Supposedly there would be a huge market for such a film because it would be showing the real thing.

As of this writing, authorities have never discovered a true snuff film, rumors to the contrary. There are some twisted simulations of snuff movies, e.g., *Flower of Flesh and Blood*, which supposedly so freaked out actor Charlie Sheen that he turned over a copy to the FBI, only to learn it was a fake, and the 1976 piece of junk *Snuff*, which at the time was rumored to contain actual footage of a murder but was in reality just a crummy repackaging of a 1971 movie called *Slaughter*.

There have also been rumors about serial killers such as John Wayne Gacy, "Son of Sam" or Jeffrey Dahmer filming or taping themselves in the act of murder. Charles Manson and his wild-eyed family also were rumored to have made some home movies of their victims. Fortunately, no such movies exist, though there have been cases of killers who have made videotapes of their victims *before* violence was committed, videotapes that, of course, were valuable pieces of evidence in subsequent trials. About 10 years ago, a couple of clowns from Virginia posted an advertisement on an Internet bulletin board, in which they said they were looking for a young boy to be tortured and killed on camera. When the men were arrested and charged with plotting a kidnapping and murder, they claimed it was all a sick joke, but they ended up serving time for their little prank.

To date, there is no documented evidence of a snuff movie, though in 1998, police in Scotland took possession of several "squish movies," in which women in skimpy garments and high heels were seen stomping frogs, mice, and insects to death.

**UL Footnote:** *8mm* is not the first mainstream Hollywood film to use a snuff movie as a plot device. In *52 Pick-Up*, a John Frankenheimer film based on an Elmore Leonard novel, businessman Roy Scheider is kidnapped and taken to a remote warehouse, where he is made to watch an amateur movie of his mistress (Kelly Preston) as she is strapped to a chair and gunned down. Adding to Scheider's horror is his realization that he's sitting in the exact same spot shown on the movie, and the blood on the wall behind him is still fresh.

Chapter Four

# LAWFULLY WEDDED LEGENDS

The wedding experience is fraught with fear, concern, anxiety, trepidation, nervousness, family pressure, financial concerns, the potential for great humiliation, and, oh yes, love. I've never been married, but I've attended dozens of weddings and I've seen hundreds of friends go through the agonizing, tedious, time-consuming, and nerve-wracking ordeal that is the pre-nuptial preparation ritual. The negotiations over who will be invited and who will be snubbed, the efforts to keep the cost of the reception low, the debates about wedding bands, entree selections, bridesmaids' dresses, the fights, the tears, and the second thoughts...

No wonder most urban legends about weddings and honeymoons are tales of great humiliation, lasting embarrassment, and/or horrible pain. The prospective brides and grooms who hear these stories can't help but feel better about their own situation...

# *The philandering groom*

This dramatic confrontation has unfolded at hundreds of wedding rehearsal dinners over the last decade, if we're to believe all of the versions of this story in circulation. Sometimes the incident is said to have taken place during the exchange of vows or at the reception, but it usually occurs at the rehearsal dinner, one or two nights before the ceremony.

Imagine the jovial scene at the rehearsal dinner. Picture the bride and groom and everyone in the wedding party laughing, crying, hugging, and sharing great stories over a terrific meal in the cozy back room of a popular restaurant. It's the kind of night that delivers memories for a lifetime.

After dinner, as the staff brings out clean plates for dessert, which will be served shortly, the bride wants to make an announcement.

"If I can just have everyone's attention for a moment," she says as she lightly taps her spoon against her glass.

The room grows quiet. This is an unusual and unexpected development, especially considering the bride's normally reserved demeanor. She's a painfully shy girl who is just not the type to give speeches unless it's absolutely necessary.

"First of all, I want to thank you all for coming," says the bride. "I know some of you have journeyed a long way to be at my wedding, and that will always mean a lot to me.

"There are some people I want to thank. First of all I'd like to express my gratitude to my parents for always being there for me. And my future in-laws, who have treated me like their own daughter from the moment I began dating their son.

"I'd also like to thank my brothers and sisters. I know I haven't always been the easiest person to live with, but I really do love you guys."

There are tears welling in the bride's eyes. Her mom and her grandmother are beginning to sniffle, as they beam proudly at their wonderful daughter. They know it's not easy for her to speak in front of a crowd, and she's doing such a wonderful job of expressing her emotions.

"Lastly," says the bride, "I want to thank my maid-of-honor, who has been my best friend for so long."

She turns to her best friend and continues: "That's right, thank you so much...for sleeping with my fiancé!"

Grandma gasps in horror. The groom's father stands and bellows, "This is an outrage!" The groom says, "Honey, you're making a huge mistake." The maid of honor says, "What are you talking about?"

"You know damn well what I'm talking about," says the bride. "And if any of you doubt my word, why don't you take a look at the little surprise taped to the bottom of your dessert plates!"

With that, the bride runs out of the room, weeping, as everyone else turns over their plates and sees a graphic photo of the bride's best friend and her fiancé making love. The bride had hired a private investigator to check out her suspicions about the two of them—suspicions that turned out to be all too true.

Needless to say, the wedding is called off, and the heart-broken bride never speaks again to her so-called best friend or her ex-fiancé. The two cheating lovers eventually move out of town and get married to each other, but the union only lasted a couple of years before they were divorced.

Sometimes it's the groom who is the wronged party, as in this version that was posted on the Internet:

There was a huge wedding, with at least 400 guests. At the reception, the groom told the band to stop playing, and he jumped up on stage and grabbed the microphone. He's a funny guy who loves the spotlight, and everyone figured he'd tell some of his favorite jokes and thank everybody for coming.

"To show my appreciation to all of you, I've arranged it so that everyone here receives a special gift," he said. "If you'll reach under your chairs, you'll find a manila envelope taped to the bottom. I'd like everyone to find their envelope and then we'll open them together at the count of three, okay?"

There was much rustling and laughter as the 400 guests reached under their chairs and found the envelopes.

"All right, everybody ready?" said the groom. "Then here we go...One, two, three!"

First there was the sound of 400 envelopes ripping open. Then there was the sound of silence, as 400 people found themselves looking at photos of the bride and the best man in a compromising position. The groom had long suspected the bride and his best buddy of having an affair, and he had hired a private investigator to tail them. The photo had been taken just a week before the wedding.

The groom turned to the best man and said, "To hell with you. You can have her." Then he turned to the bride and said, "And to hell with you too. I want a divorce."

With that, he walked out of the reception hall.

# The videotaped theft

These days, no wedding goes untaped, shot by either a professional outfit or an uncle with his video camera. Walk into any wedding reception in America, and you're sure to see at least one guy working the room like he's Martin Scorsese's cinematographer, sticking his camera in everyone's faces and interviewing people for the three hour-plus opus.

For all the hard work done by these would-be auteurs, who really wants to watch the final product? Wedding videos are only entertaining when awful or embarrassing behavior is caught on tape. For instance, when somebody's obnoxious 12-year-old nephew siphons a few ounces from Grandma's whiskey sour when she isn't looking, or the camera catches the groom's married brother cupping the rear end of a giggling bridesmaid, or you surreptitiously pick up a conversation at a table where they're making bets about how long the marriage will last.

Or, a thief is nabbed on tape, as in the following urban legend, which has been in circulation ever since the advent of the home videocam in the 1980s.

The scene is a reception in a popular banquet hall, with 300 guests celebrating the union of a fine, upstanding young couple. There's a table at the entrance for people to leave gifts, but most of the guests have come bearing envelopes containing cash or checks, and they hand these envelopes directly to the bride, who stuffs them into a silk bag which she leaves at her place setting as she mingles with guests.

"That's an awful lot of money to leave unattended," says her maid of honor, but the bride laughs and says, "Come on, it's a wedding, we know everybody here. It's not like someone's going to steal it."

She's right, the bag isn't stolen—but someone reaches in and steals the envelopes, replacing them with a bunch of envelopes containing nothing but strips of paper. Because the heft of the bag feels the same, the bride doesn't discover the shocking theft until well after the reception is over.

"There were 300 guests at that wedding, plus all the people who worked for the banquet hall," she says to her new husband. "We're *never* going to find out who did this!"

The next morning, before they leave for their honeymoon, they get a call from the groom's brother, who had spent the entire wedding running around with his video camera, shooting everything in sight.

"I was up all night watching the tape," he says. "You guys better come over. There's something you need to see."

The couple hurries over to the guy's house, and he pops in the tape, with the video cued to the moment of truth.

"This was when everyone was on the dance floor for 'Celebration,'" he says. "Well, almost everyone. Look in the background, at the head table..."

As the bride and groom lean forward, the groom's brother hits the pause button and then begins to advance the tape frame by frame. A man in a tuxedo enters the picture and quickly removes the contents of the bride's bag, replacing them with the worthless, paper-stuffed envelopes.

"Oh my God," sobs the bride...for it's her very own father.

I've heard the "videotaped theft" story a dozen times, but it's always in the classic "friend of a friend" vein. No one has ever provided me with the names of any of the principals, let alone the chance to view the tape.

# *Wedding quickies*

L et's flip through the urban legend wedding photo album and gaze at a few snapshots of popular ULs about brides and grooms and wacky wedding guests.

## The wrong Robin Hood

Kevin Costner's *Robin Hood: Prince of Thieves* was a box office hit that spawned a No. 1 hit record: "Everything I Do (I Do For You)" by the Canadian rocker Bryan Adams. It's one of those bombastic rock ballads that becomes a staple at proms, homecoming dances—and weddings. In fact, many a bride in the 1990s has asked that the song be played in lieu of the wedding march itself.

And so it was that a young bride told the church organist, a middle-aged fellow, of her desire for "the theme from *Robin Hood*" to be played as she walks down the aisle.

"But I'm not sure if that's appropriately dignified for such a solemn occasion," said the somewhat confused organist.

"Look, do you know the song?" said the bride.

"Well, sure, but—"

"But nothing. Just play it, okay? It's what I want. The theme from *Robin Hood*. Do you think you can handle that?"

The organist shrugged his shoulders. "If you insist."

"I insist."

On her wedding day, the bride never looked more beautiful. She stood at the back of the church, fighting the tears as she waited to hear the song she had specially chosen for the occasion...

The organist began to play—not the Bryan Adams song, but the bouncy, uptempo theme from the 1960 *Robin Hood* TV series.

Titters erupted throughout the church. The bride frantically tried to signal to the organist that he was playing the wrong song, but he was so into it he never even looked up. She had no choice but to walk (rather, gallop) down the aisle as the cheesy adventure song blared through the church.

## The X-rated couple

Another videotape caper. In this one, the couple has such a great time on their honeymoon that they return to the same resort—the same room, even—to celebrate their one-year anniversary. In order to get into the mood, they turn on the hotel's X-rated movie channel, and discover that they're the stars in the feature of the day! Someone had secretly videotaped them on their honeymoon, and their sexual antics had been duplicated and shown in a hundred hotels across the country.

Needless to say, the couple filed a major lawsuit and received a huge settlement.

## The heel in the grate

Bridesmaid gets heel caught in wedding-aisle grate and leaves it there, her bare foot fortunately concealed by her long dress. Helpful groomsman tries to pry the shoe free, but he succeeds only in lifting the entire grate, with the heel still caught. Next up is the bride, who falls right through the opening and disappears.

This incident was re-created for the movie *The Glass-Bottom Boat* (but in a NASA training facility, not at a wedding). Doris Day's heel gets caught in a grate, Rod Taylor picks up the grate with the shoe still attached, and Dick Martin (of Rowan & Martin fame) is the hapless sucker who falls into the hole.

Chapter Five

# RUMORS IN THE AIR TONIGHT

Dave Matthews isn't e-mailing his fans to help a dying young girl. However, a host of theories and stories still suggests that he is. We'll look at that nonsense here, along with a number of other popular urban myths about pop music, including the eerie origins of the Phil Collins hit, "In the Air Tonight." You might have thought of it as nothing but an overplayed pop standard, but wait until you hear who the song is really about...

# A killer
## "In the Air Tonight"

With the possible exception of James Brown's "I Feel Good," perhaps no pop song in history has been used in as many commercials, TV shows, and movies as "In the Air Tonight" by Phil Collins. With its hypnotic, synthesized opening, haunting echo-effect lyrics, and percussion-driven crescendo, it's the perfect mood piece for any number of commercials or dramatic scenes, from ads for Michelob beer to the original music-video dramatic series *Miami Vice*. Collins probably could have made a pretty decent living in the late 1980s and early 1990s just from the royalties generated by that one song.

I always figured "In the Air Tonight" was the story of a jealous man telling his lover he knows she's been unfaithful:

*And I was there and I saw what you did, saw it with my own two eyes*
*So you can wipe off that grin, I know where you've been*
*It's all been a pack of lies*
*And I can feel it coming in the air tonight...*

In 1992, Collins was quoted in *Parade* Magazine as saying the song was about the breakup of his first marriage. Not that this rather ordinary explanation for the genesis (get it?) of "In the Air Tonight" did anything to dispel the long-running rumors about the *real* origin of the song. The details vary greatly from telling to telling, but the common theme is that Collins witnessed a death or tragedy of some great magnitude, and used that raw experience as material for the song. He then belted out "In the Air Tonight" in a passionate concert attended by the wrongdoer named in the song.

In one version, Collins is walking along the beach while his brother is out on Collins' boat. Some sort of accident occurs and Collin's brother falls overboard, but Collins is much too far away to do anything about it. Another boat cruises past, but the person on that boat does nothing to save Collins' brother, and the poor man dies. The other boat speeds away without giving a statement to authorities, but Collins manages to catch the boat's name before it disappears from view. With the help of private detectives, he learns the identity of the boat captain, as well as the man's address and many other bits of personal information. He patiently waits a year, and then, with the help of a cooperative radio station and a friendly concert promoter, he fixes it so that the boat's owner "wins" 10th row tickets to see Phil Collins live.

That night at the show, Collins says he's dedicating a new song, "In the Air Tonight," to his brother, who died tragically exactly one year ago. (He doesn't say how.) Halfway through the song, a spotlight shines directly on the boat captain, as Collins sings directly to him:

> *So you can wipe off that grin, I know where you've been*
> *It's all been a pack of lies!*

The guilty fan realizes the song is about him, and he has a breakdown right then and there as the song kicks into its climax, with Collins furiously pounding the drums and the crowd going crazy.

In another version, the concert scenario is essentially the same—only this time the lucky winner isn't someone who didn't save Phil Collins' brother from drowning, it's a rapist or a killer who committed a crime while the singer looked on helplessly from a hidden spot nearby. Only when the thug hears the lyrics does he realize a famous songwriter has not only witnessed the crime but has set it to music. (Sometimes the rapist and/or killer's victim is Collins' own wife; sometimes it's a stranger.)

In yet another telling, Collins is mugged on the beach and chases the man into the water. The mugger gets caught in the undertow and cries out for help, but the famous singer stands by and does nothing.

> *Well if you told me you were drowning, I would not lend a hand,*
> *I've seen your face before my friend, but I don't know if you know who I am.*

The song is supposedly about his own feelings of guilt over the mugger's death.

For the record, Phil Collins does not have a brother who drowned, nor was he the witness to some unspeakably horrible crime, nor did he refuse to help a sinking mugger. By all accounts, "In the Air Tonight" is about love gone wrong.

# The Dave Matthews chain letter

Every once in a while I'll read about a celebrity who likes to go online and anonymously surf around the Internet under one of those goofy AOL names like Muffy321 or Smelly874, maybe even visiting their own Web sites, chat rooms, and message boards. I can readily attest that it's an irresistible temptation; as a newspaper columnist and TV and radio commentator in Chicago, I've often been the subject of such discussion groups on the Internet, and I must admit I've visited those areas to see what people are saying. A couple of times I've even joined in the conversation, if only to set the record straight when I read something that is just plain incorrect. But even when I'm just lurking about, it's a strange sensation when you see that someone you've never met, someone who does not have to identify himself or herself in any way, can write something negative.

Imagine then what it must be like to be *really* famous, on a global level, and to have access to all these instant Internet conversations about your career, your love life, your family, etc. If a celebrity did respond to you, either via a direct e-mail or bulletin board posting, how would you know it wasn't an impostor? In the early days of the Internet, before most of the good log-ons were taken, anyone could have grabbed screen names such as Hanks222 or Elton432 and proclaimed themselves to be Tom Hanks or Elton John. There was no way of knowing.

Be suspicious, then, if you receive an e-mail from singer/ songwriter Dave Matthews. Over the last couple of years, Matthews (or, to be more accurate, somebody claiming to be him) has been a ubiquitous presence on the e-mail circuit with a letter that has been copied and forwarded thousands upon thousands of times. I've had this sent to me at least a half-dozen times; in order to get to the text of the letter itself, I always have to scroll down past countless blocks of screen names and little attached messages imploring me to "Keep going, it's worth it!"

I also see a lot of notes like this:

Subect: fwd

Hey everybody, this is SO UNBELIEVABLY SAD! please read this and send it on to all your friends. if dave matthews can take the time so can you! a child's life could be at stake.

And:

Subj: HELP A DYING KID

please keep scrolling and read the message at the bottom of this letter, it could save someone's life! this means you, all of you! don't let me down!

Finally, the letter itself:

Hi! This is Dave Matthews. That's right, Dave Matthews from the Dave Matthews Band. I want to thank everyone for supporting the band by buying our records and coming to see us in concert, but that's not why I'm writing to you today. No, this is something much more important, which is why I'm writing this myself. I just got America Online a while ago, and my secretary will send you my screen name if you send this to at least five more people who are online. The reason I am doing this is because a little girl needs our help, and I thought I could use my fame to help out this sick little girl.

She has only six months to live, and as her dying wish she wanted to send a chain letter telling everyone to live their life to the fullest, since she never will. She'll never make it to the prom, she'll never graduate from high school, she'll never get married or have a family of her own. But by you sending this to as many people as possible, you can give her and her family a little hope, because with every name that this is sent to, the American Cancer Society will donate 3 cents per name to her treatment and recovery plan.

If you're too selfish or lazy to spend a few minutes forwarding this to a few of your friends, just remember: This could be you someday.

Your friend,

Dave Matthews

The chain letter, supposedly written by the rock star, contains exact fragments of other bogus fundraising e-mails authored by fictional cancer patients "Tamara Martin," "David Lawitts," and "Jessica Mydek" among others. It's also reminiscent of the Craig Shergold letter, examined earlier in this book. When you read the letter closely, you realize it makes little sense. First we're told the little girl is dying and she wants us all to appreciate our good fortune to be healthy. Then we're told if we pass on the letter, a donation will be made to assist in her "treatment and recovery."

Not to mention the fact that the American Cancer Society is not in the business of doling out money for treatment based on who gets the most "hits" on the Internet. Says Bud Jones, vice president of communications and government affairs for the organization: "The American Cancer Society is not in the business of giving away money. None of this is true. In fact, the Dave Matthews rumor is a variation on a theme. There's a new one cropping up lately about a doctor writing a similar letter about a kid and sending it around. The doctor named in the letter is an actual person, but when we contacted him, he said he had nothing to do with the letter."

# *J. Lo gets the heave-ho*

After collecting and examining urban legends for nearly 15 years, I like to think I've got decent radar for UL's, hoaxes, scams, phony petitions, and e-mailed myths. My rule has always been, if something sounds too good, too delicious, too ironic, to be true, that's because it *is* too good to be true.

But every once in a while, real life trumps the urban myth.

In the spring of 2001, I came across two sets of e-mails that had been copied and forwarded endlessly around the globe. I was quite certain that both of these were pure myth—but it turned out that one was absolutely authentic. See if *you* can tell which one contains actual correspondence, and which is pure fiction.

## The Tao of J. Lo

A friend of mine who covers the entertainment field once had an interview scheduled with Jennifer Lopez in a hotel suite in Chicago. My friend arrived on time, camera crew in tow, and was asked to wait downstairs while Lopez got ready.

Three hours later, the interview started.

It's that kind of behavior that has led observers to call Lopez the ultimate diva of her time—among other things. Consider this report from the May 2, 2001, edition of the entertainment Web site *Buzzle.com*:

Superstars that are difficult to please and that make eccentric demands are certainly nothing new to the Hollywood landscape, but industry scene watchers are labeling Jennifer Lopez as one of the most difficult stars to please, ever. As stories of unprovoked tirades and a 'holier than thou' attitude continue to pile up, so does the size of Puffy's former sweetheart's security force...

Jennifer's security guards have standing orders that no one is to make eye contact or speak directly to the Latin diva. Producers and wardrobe people must obey the Lopez Rules, which include her insistence on having a particular type of bra...all in a day's work for the Princess of Pomposity.

With a reputation like that, it's little wonder that Lopez would surround herself with people who display copious amounts of attitude when representing their client. Consider the following e-mail thread between a publicist for the giant firm of Rogers and Cowan who represents Lopez, and an executive with Warner Bros., as they battle over the promotion of the Lopez-starring thriller, "Angel Eyes."

From: Martha Hudson, Warner Bros.
To: Lucille LeSueur, Rogers & Cowan
Yes, we got your fax...I thought Jennifer's rep said she wanted to do anything to promote this movie.
Martha Hudson
Publicity Manager, Warner Bros.

From: Lucille LeSueur
To: Martha Hudson
Of course, she wants to do "anything." (Thought you said you got the fax.) She merely wants to meet you halfway.

From: Martha Hudson
To: Lucille LeSueur

Lucy, how can I put this? (I suppose I should phone, but I'm too upset!) According to this fax, you're asking us to pull all the one-sheets, posters, and prints of the movie in order to bill Jennifer as "J. Lo" instead of her (expletive deleted) God-given name. This is NOT going "halfway"—unless she intends to pay for the millions out of her own pocket. We are talking about a movie that opens in two weeks! The junket is tomorrow!!! Are you guys smoking crack over there with Robert Downey Jr.?

The bottom line (and I've got backup on this): She signed onto this project as "Jennifer Lopez." She—so help me—is going to be billed as "Jennifer Lopez." We can't help it if she's decided to get a diva transplant.

From: Lucille LeSueur
To: Martha Hudson

Okay, I'm going to do you a big favor, Martha. I'm not going to repeat what you've said to J. Lo. But only because I don't want to see her go to jail FOR RIPPING YOUR ORGANS OUT WITH HER BARE HANDS! I simply can't believe the lack of respect here. Maybe you can play these games with "James" Caviezel (or is it Jim? Gee, I guess he can't make up his mind either.) But J. Lo clearly is no "James/Jim" Caviezel. She is the world's preeminent female celebrity. She has more talent in her ass than most people have in their tiny finger. J. Lo is not just an actress. She is not just a singer. She is not just a celebrity. She is a movement. (Why do I even have to say this?) She feels extra-determined that "Jennifer Lopez" isn't where her movement is these days. She is "J. Lo."

From: Martha Hudson
To: Lucille LeSueur

I'd like to see "J. Lo" try to rip out my organs. I hear my liver would grow back anyway. Which is more than I can say for her movie career after this piece of —— opens.

From: Lucille LeSueur
To: Martha Hudson

This note is to inform you that J. Lo has taken ill and will be unable to attend Saturday's press junket at the Four Seasons in Beverly Hills.

She respectfully sends her regrets.

From: Martha Hudson
TO: Lucille LeSueur

Dearest Lucy: Kiss kiss. We're sorry to hear about poor Jennifer Lopez. At least we won't blow our kissing-and-fawning budget tomorrow. We'll need it for the Travolta movie "Swordfish" coming up.

## Everybody Wang Chung Tonight!

You'd think by now that today's Internet-savvy young professionals would know better than to send anything via e-mail that they don't want the whole world to see. Alas, the lessons keep coming. Just ask Peter Chung, a former Merrill Lynch employee who took a job with the Seoul, South Korea branch of the Carlyle Group (a private equity firm) in the spring of 2001 and sent an e-mail to 11 of his former co-workers, bragging about his new life. Chung's new employers had set him up with a six-figure salary and a three-bedroom apartment, and the 24-year-old Princeton graduate was having the time of his life—as he bragged about in his e-letter to the boys back home:

So I've been in Korea for about a week and a half and what can I say, LIFE IS GOOD. I've got a brand spanking new 2,000 sq. foot, 3-bedroom apartment with a 200 sq. ft. terrace running the entire length of my apartment with a view overlooking Korea's main river and nightline…Why do I need three bedrooms? Good question. The main bedroom is for my queen size bed, where CHUNG is going to —— every hot chick in Korea over the next two years. (Five down, 1 billion left to go!) The second bedroom is for my harem of chickies and the third bedroom is for all you ——— when you come out to visit my ass in Korea. I go out to Korea's finest clubs, bars and lounges pretty much every other night on the weekdays and every day on the weekends…I know I was a stud in NYC but I pretty much get about, on average, 5-8 phone numbers a night and at least three hot chicks that say they want to go home with me every night I go out…I live in the same apartment building as my VP and he drives me around in his Porsche (one of three in all of Korea)…What can I say, life is good, CHUNG is KING of his domain here in Seoul…

So all you ——— better keep in touch and start making plans to come out and visit my ass ASAP. I'll show you guys an unbelievable time…

Later, CHUNG.

Both e-mails are admittedly funny in a twisted kind of way—but my initial impression was that neither had the ring of truth. The supposed exchange between the Warner Bros. PR rep and the J. Lo's person quickly disintegrates into a petty squabble that probably would have cost both these people their jobs—if they existed. Not to mention the gaps in logic. The "more talent in her ass than most people have in their tiny finger" seems like more of an insult to J. Lo—but it comes from her own rep. Nor would the publicist for a studio call her own movie "a piece of [garbage]" just because one of the stars was acting up. That would only torpedo her own career—as would the comment about John Travolta and his upcoming movie.

But the memo from the braggart, all-caps CHUNG to his pals also seems like the product of somebody's imagination. Could Princeton really produce a moron who would talk like that—and who wouldn't know enough *not* to share his idiotic delusions with the Internet world?

Actually, yes. There really is a Peter Chung, and he really did compose such a letter—and it really did get his ass fired, to borrow one of his terms.

*The New York Times* had the story on May 22, 2001:

> Paul [sic] Chung, a recently hired associate at the Carlyle Group in Seoul, Korea, was forced to resign on Friday after boasting about his sexual exploits and lavish lifestyle in an e-mail message to 11 buddies at Merrill Lynch in New York, where he used to work.
>
> Unfortunately for Mr. Chung…the message was forwarded or passed on to thousands of people on Wall Street and wound up being sent to his bosses…
>
> Reached by telephone in Seoul, Mr. Chung said: "It's devastating. I really can't comment. Sorry."

You're sorry? What about all those Korean chickies who won't be able to bask in the glory of the KING that is CHUNG?

Chung is not the first professional to send a salacious e-mail, only to see it ricochet around the world and lead to unemployment. In 2000, a woman at a British Internet provider wrote an extremely graphic series of jokes and notes to her boyfriend about a particular sex act. The cad forwarded the notes to dozens of friends, including a number of lawyers—many of whom were disciplined by their respective firms.

As for the J. Lo memos—total fiction. The Web site *ifilm.com* includes a running feature of imaginary e-mails that satirize Hollywood, and the May 16, 2001 entry was titled, "Hell hath no fury like J. Lo's magical butt." In what has become a familiar scenario, the satire was pasted onto various e-mails and launched into cyberspace, where some readers interpreted it as legitimate correspondence. The June 11 *"Intelligencer"* column of *New York* magazine's Web site reported on the mix-up:

"You'd think Jennifer Lopez's publicist would have enough work on his hands in real life. But we hear her rep, Alan Nierob, was recently besieged by calls after a fake e-mail exchange between one of 'Lopez's publicists' and a 'Warner Bros. honcho' circulated the globe…'People believed it, and we received quite a few calls,' Nierob's weary assistant confirms."

Another hint that the memo isn't authentic: Lucille LaSueur was Joan Crawford's real name.

Now, if only Chung can find work with Lopez's entourage:

"Hey buds! It's me, CHUNG, the KING of Hollywood! My new place has three bedrooms: One for me, one for J. Lo, and one for J. Lo's butt!"

# The heckling guitarist

If you put all the great reviews Grand Funk Railroad ever received in a scrapbook, it would be about as thick as a take-out menu from your favorite restaurant. Long-haired lead singer Mark Farner and his band mates sold millions of albums and churned out numerous hits such as "We're an American Band," "I'm Your Captain/Closer to Home," and a remake of Little Eva's "Locomotion" in the 1970s, but they were almost unanimously dismissed by critics and rock purists as a hack band playing to the lowest common denominator.

That's why Grand Funk Railroad is the perfect group to star in a popular urban legend. Seems the band was playing to a packed house sometime around 1972, and everyone in the crowd was going crazy—with one notable exception. The boys were distracted by the constant booing and heckling coming from a lone male voice in front of the stage. Finally, the lead guitarist grabbed the microphone between songs and said, "We're trying to do a show up here, but someone is hassling us. Tell you what: If you think you can do better, why don't you come on up here?"

"As a matter of fact I think I will!" bellows the man.

The guys in the band can't really see what's going on because of the spotlights in their eyes, but there's a great commotion as the unknown heckler makes his way to the stage and is helped up by a couple of roadies. "Can you believe the guy's actually coming up here?" says Farner.

When the heckler steps into the light, a roar of recognition surges through the crowd.

It's none other than Eric Clapton.

In January of 1997, a variation on this story was retold on the Internet:

> One night, sometime around 1970, Grand Funk had 'em packed into Detroit's Cobo Arena, but for some reason, they just couldn't connect with the audience. As they cranked out each hit, the boos got louder and louder until Mark Farner screamed at the audience, "If anybody out there can play guitar better than me, they can just come up here and do it!"
>
> Quietly, a solitary figure stepped out of the crowd, and, head bowed, made his way onto the stage. As the security guards stepped aside, he walked up to Farner, who immediately unstrapped his guitar and gave it to him. The stranger, now in the spotlight, strummed one chord and said, Hello, I'm Eric Clapton.
>
> Grand Funk slinked off the stage and turned it over to Clapton, who played solo to a manic crowd for the next two hours.

Sometimes the band in the story is the Guess Who instead of Grand Funk Railroad, but the heckling musician has always been identified as Clapton. Why Eric Clapton would be at a Grand Funk Railroad or Guess Who concert in the first place is anybody's guess, but it's safe to assume that even the Clapton of those crazy days wouldn't have been so rude as to heckle a mid-level band, nor choose to take over a concert and play for free.

Clapton's incredible guitar skills play a factor in another urban legend, in which the local pastor at a church in England politely rebuffs young Eric's offer to play some acoustic guitar during Sunday Mass, finally relenting only because he feels sorry for the lad. When Clapton does get his chance, he's beyond great, of course.

The Clapton story has also morphed into an oft-told tale about a young comic who goes on *The Tonight Show* or the *Late Show with David Letterman* and tells a story about his most embarrassing moment onstage. Seems he was playing the Comedy Store one night and was getting a pretty good response from the audience, with the exception of one clown who kept stepping on his punch lines. The comic was of course blinded by the spotlight, but he started bantering with the heckler until he ran out of material and said in exasperation, "Look, if you think you're so funny, why don't you come up here and I'll sit in the audience?"

"Don't mind if I do!" replied the unruly customer—who turned out to be none other than Robin Williams.

Or Eddie Murphy, as I've heard it told on other occasions.

**UL FOOTNOTE:** This story was chronicled by the *Chicago Tribune* and was confirmed by dozens of eyewitnesses. Some years ago, a pickup basketball game on the south side of Chicago was interrupted by a brash talker who wanted a piece of the action. In this instance, though, there was no mistaking the heckler. It was Michael Jordan, who played in a couple of spirited games with the talented street kids and then sped off in his car. Jordan also regularly participated in pickup games in some of the more exclusive downtown health clubs in Chicago, and those who played against him said he was as competitive in a game of half-court hoops with a bunch of amateurs as he was in the NBA finals.

# "You Oughta Know"
## who this song's about

Alanis Morisette, the former teenage actor from Canada, exploded onto the music scene in 1995 with the release of her third album, *Jagged Little Pill*, which has sold something like 20 million copies worldwide. The first single, "You Oughta Know," was a savage, bitter story of a young woman who lashes out at her ex-boyfriend for quickly finding a new lover.

*Did you forget about me, Mister Duplicity?*
*I hate to bug you in the middle of dinner*
*It was a slap in my face how quickly I was replaced*
*Are you thinking of me when you f\*\*k her?*

"You Oughta Know" has been the subject of much speculation about whether or not the song has a real-life inspiration. In a 1995 interview with the *Toronto Sun*, the 21-year-old Morissette acknowledged the existence of such a muse.

"I haven't heard from him," she told the paper. "And I don't think he knows. Which sort of says a lot about him. The ironic thing is, if anybody questions whether it's them I'm writing about, that means something in and of itself. People who were kind and honest and full of integrity throughout the process of making this album wouldn't question whether they were in that song because they would know."

Two male celebrities have been pegged as the man refer-
enced in "You Oughta Know": Bob Saget, and Dave Coulier
of *Full House* fame.

I've heard from a few Morissette fans who swear Saget is
the ex-boyfriend targeted in the song. But they've got it mixed
up. The Coulier theory is much more plausible.

"It wasn't Bob Saget. It was that other guy on *Full House*,
the one who was funny and had blond hair," posted one fan on
the Internet. "He was on a radio station in Boston and admitted for the first time that he was the person Alanis sang about
in her song. He got some girl pregnant while he was dating her."

Another post:

> You Oughta Know' was written about Dave Coolea
> [*sic*]...from *Full House*. They used to date, then he
> dumped her. I heard this straight from his mouth on
> K-ROQ [on the] Kevin and Bean morning show. They
> found it out, called him, and he confirmed it's all true!

The weird thing is, Morissette really did date Coulier. In
the early 1990s, when she was fairly well known in Canada because of her work on the series *You Can't do That on Television* and her pop career, Morissette was hired by the NHL's
new franchise, the Ottawa Senators, to entertain the crowds.
That led to her being asked to sing "O Canada" at the 1992
NHL All-Star game in Montreal. It was there that she met
Coulier, a rabid hockey fan and a pretty fair amateur player
who often participated in charity games. The relationship reportedly ended because at 19, Morissette felt she was too young
to start a family.

Cut to a few years later, when "You Oughta Know" topped
the charts. Morissette was now recast as the quintessential
angry young woman, thrashing about the stage as she sang
about the man who left her for another woman. This led to
much speculation about the identity of the man in the song.

Among those mentioned were Mike Peluso of the Ottawa Senators, and *Friends* star Matt LeBlanc, who appeared in a Morissette video before she became a big star.

Leslie Howe, a longtime Morissette friend and sometime collaborator, was so upset that his name was bandied about that he called the *Ottawa Star* to deny he was the inspiration for the song. "Alanis and I were friends and worked together professionally," he told the paper. "But we certainly never dated."

But the name mentioned most often is Dave Coulier's. In Paul Cantin's biography, *Alanis Morissette*, the singer says this about the rumor: "I'm not going to deny or say yes to it because I think it is wrong. I sort of laugh at it. That was a most public relationship, and it is a predictable answer...The truth is I am never going to tell who it is about." Cantin quotes Morissette as saying it would be unnecessarily cruel to reveal the identity of the man in the song. "If it was written for the sake of revenge, Lord knows, I would be plastering his picture everywhere. And I would never do that, because I have too much respect for him."

The E! Web site tries to refute the Coulier story: "Although [Coulier] still likes to think of himself as the muse who sparked Morissette, that place in history is reserved for another old Canuck boyfriend."

# *The dark side of Oz*

As with the great majority of urban legends, it's impossible to determine exactly when this one started, but we can surmise with some confidence *how* it got started. Somebody was really stoned, and they popped in Pink Floyd's *Dark Side of the Moon* on the stereo while *The Wizard of Oz* began playing on the VCR. Our unknown stoner/scholar takes a massive hit on his bong and settles back into his bean bag chair for a multi-sensory experience. As the MGM lion roars, side one of *Dark Side of the Moon* begins. At first the viewer doesn't notice anything strange, but as the movie and the music play on, he gets an eerie feeling: They're somehow synchronized!

The parallels are too accurate and too often to be attributed to mere coincidence. In chronological order, here are some of the connections:

> ➣ In one of the opening scenes, Dorothy is looking at the ground as we hear the words, "look around and choose your ground."

> ➣ Dorothy opts not to sit on a bench as we hear the words, "Don't sit down..."

> ➣ A synthesizer that sounds like an airplane is heard on "Dark Side of the Moon" at the precise moment when Dorothy is looking at the sky.

➤ We hear bells on the album at the exact moment when Margaret Hamilton rides in on her bicycle, ringing the bike's bell.

➤ Dorothy is seen running just as the band sings, "No one told you when to run..."

➤ During the song "Pulse," a woman's voice can be heard whispering very softly. Crank up the volume and you'll hear what she's saying: "I never said I was afraid of Dorothy."

➤ When the tornado plunks Dorothy into Munchkin Land and the screen changes from black-and-white to color, the cash registers of "Money" kick in. This is a sly reference to the Yellow Brick Road, and its bricks of gold.

➤ As the Good Witch's bubble enters the picture, we hear the words "goody good bulls**t."

➤ When the Wicked Witch makes her first appearance, we hear the words, "black, black."

➤ During the song "Us and Them," we hear the words "and who knows which is which and who is who" just as Dorothy is confused, trying to figure out which of these bizarre characters are the good guys and which ones are dangerous.

➤ The first time we see the Scarecrow, Pink Floyd's "Brain Damage" starts playing. The Scarecrow is dancing as we hear the words, "The lunatic is on the grass."

➤ Dorothy and the Scarecrow are about to enter the dark forest as we hear the words, "See you on the dark side of the moon..."

➤ The heartbeat sound effect heard at the end of "Dark Side of the Moon" kicks in just as Dorothy is beating on the Tin Man's chest.

End of album. But obviously the movie isn't over, which is one of the problems with this urban legend. *Dark Side of the Moon* has a running time less than half that of *The Wizard of Oz*, but some of the "Pink Freud" legends I've heard continue to draw comparisons between sections of the album and scenes from the film right until the moment when Dorothy returns home. What are you supposed to do—re-cue the album?

That's another serious flaw in this admittedly entertaining theory. In 1973, when *Dark Side of the Moon* was recorded, the only copies of *The Wizard of Oz* available would have been theatrical prints. While it's theoretically possible that Roger Waters, David Gilmour, and company could have arranged to have a print of the film playing while they composed the album, such a complicated feat would be much easier in the modern era of videocassettes, laser discs, DVDs, and digital technology. To attempt to synchronize an album to the flickering images on a silver screen would seem to be a nearly impossible task, even for the creative geniuses in Pink Floyd.

As far as I was able to determine, none of the notoriously media-shy members of Floyd have ever commented on this urban legend, which didn't surface until about two decades after the album was released. However, rock scholar Timothy White, the author of the definitive biography of the band, says there's absolutely no truth to the story.

In the interest of research, I forced myself to watch *The Wizard of Oz* again with the sound turned down and a CD of *Dark Side of the Moon* cued up. I don't smoke dope but I do drink Red Stripe beer, and I sipped a couple just to get into a more accepting mood. Weirdly enough, most of the episodes described above actually did occur, and I have to admit I got the chills a couple of times, like when Dorothy knocked on the Tin Man's chest and a heartbeat comes out of the CD player. We can chalk up some of these Floyd/Oz parallels to coincidence and others to wishful thinking on the part of the interpreters, but the whole thing is a bit freaky.

# The "Love Rollercoaster" death scream

When I was about 14, some of my favorite albums in the whole world came from the funky rhythm and soul group known as the Ohio Players. Along with groundbreaking bands such as Sly & the Family Stone; Earth, Wind & Fire; and Kool & the Gang, they produced a kind of *Soul Train*-meets-Big-Band sound that was perfect for the era. Their biggest hit of all was "Love Rollercoaster," the 1975 release that sailed to the top of the Billboard charts. I remember listening to "Love Rollercoaster" in somebody's basement when a buddy of mine told a hair-raising story about the recording of the song—in particular, the musical bridge where you hear a twanging guitar and what sounds like a woman screaming.

"Someone gave the producer an audio tape of a woman actually being murdered, and he thought it would be cool to put it in the song," my pal claimed. "The Ohio Players didn't know this; they just thought some actress had done the recording. By the time they learned the truth, it was too late—the song was already playing on the radio. But in protest, they said they would never play "Love Rollercoaster" in concert or on TV shows like *Soul Train* or *Midnight Special*."

In college several years later, I heard another take on the "Love Rollercoaster" death scream. "The Ohio Players got a tape recording of a woman falling to her death on the Blue Streak rollercoaster ride in Cedar Point Amusement Park in Ohio, and they used it on the song," I was told.

More preposterous was the notion that the scream "accidentally" showed up on the song. Supposedly the band recorded the song in guitarist/vocalist Jimmy "Sugarfoot" Bonner's apartment, and a murder took place next door. The scream was recorded by the sound engineers, the band isolated the sound and increased the volume, and they kept it on the record because it perfectly fit the song.

Even the naked woman from the *Honey* album cover was brought into the legend. In the cover photo, she's kneeling atop a sheet of Fiberglass; according to the UL, when the honey on her body connected with the synthetic material, it became as sticky as Superglue, and her skin was spontaneously fused to the sheet. The act of ripping her legs free created terrible abrasions, and she was scarred for life, thus ruining her career as a nude model. Several weeks later, the Ohio Players were doing some mixing on "Love Rollercoaster" when the hysterical model burst through the door of the recording studio with a gun and threatened to kill them for destroying her livelihood. Before she could get off any shots, the band's manager stabbed her to death. The mikes were on and tape was rolling during this confrontation, and the woman's final screams of anguish were used on the record.

Nearly a quarter-century after "Love Rollercoaster" was released, the myth got a boost from the movie *Urban Legend*. In the movie, a bunch of college kids who weren't even born when "Love Rollercoaster" came out are playing it at a party, and a guy tries to impress a chick by telling her the UL about the song.

The truth is that the scream comes from a vocalist who was simply trying to hit the highest note possible, emulating what it might sound like if someone were on a really scary rollercoaster.

The best explanation for the whole "death scream" rumor was that it was apparently started by some long-forgotten DJ who made a joke about it back in '75, and it's taken on a life of its own ever since. As Ohio Player drummer Jimmy "Diamond" Williams once said, "People were asking us, 'Did you kill this chick in the studio?' The band took a vow of silence because that makes you sell more records."

But listening to a digitally re-mastered recording of "Love Rollercoaster" through headphones, I have to admit the hairs on my arm stood up when I heard that scream. Maybe it's the resonance of the woman's voice, maybe it's the way the scream was mixed in, maybe it's the accumulation of all those stories over the years, but it sure gave me the creeps.

# *Other chart-topping legends*

Without commercial interruptions, let's play some other music-related urban legends back to back to back:

## The *Bat Out of Hell* will

Millions of fans think Meat Loaf's multi-platinum album *Bat Out of Hell*, featuring the over-the-top classics "Two Out of Three Ain't Bad" and "Paradise By the Dashboard Light," is right up there with the Beatles' *White Album*, Led Zeppelin *IV,* and The Who's *Tommy* as one of the greatest albums in the history of rock.

Millions of others think it's worse than Muzak in a supermarket on a Saturday afternoon.

From such loathing springs the urban legend about the eccentric millionaire who dies and has it put in his will that his chief beneficiary, who apparently hates Meat Loaf, must listen to *Bat Out of Hell* in its entirety *every day for the rest of his life*, or he won't receive his monthly inheritance check.

One question: Who was supposed to monitor the beneficiary's behavior every day to make sure he listened to the album? For the monitor's sake, I hope he *loves* Meat Loaf.

## "Hey hey we're the Mansons"?

As you probably know, the infamous mass murderer Charles Manson was a would-be musician who recorded a number of demo songs and even lived for a time with Beach Boys drummer Dennis Wilson. Tinny-sounding Manson recordings occasionally are played by "controversial" DJs who want to show how outrageous they can be. In that same vein, rockers Guns 'N' Roses included a Manson song on their album *The Spaghetti Incident*.

Manson desperately wanted success as a pop singer. He even auditioned to be on *The Monkees* TV show—or so the UL goes.

In 1965, *Variety* ran an advertisement from producers Bob Rafelson and Bert Schneider, who were looking for "four insane boys, aged 17-21," to audition for a new TV series about an American version of a Beatlesque band, The Monkees. There were more than 400 respondents, including a young Stephen Stills, who didn't make the final cut. A clean-cut Manson was also reportedly among the would-be musicians hoping *The Monkees* would be his big break, but Manson (like Stills and future stars Harry Nilsson and Danny Hutton of Three Dog Night) was deemed to be not quite as talented as Mickey Dolenz, Mike Nesmith, Peter Tork, and Davey Jones.

This has become an accepted part of Manson lore, repeated on radio shows and TV shows, and cited as fact in newspaper articles. To wit, a *Chicago Tribune* article from Feb. 19, 1999 about an offbeat Chicago theater group doing a musical based on Manson's life, includes this background information on Manson's colorful insanity: "He hung out with Dennis Wilson of the Beach Boys [who allegedly wanted to become part of the Manson family], tried to get Terry Melcher—Doris Day's record-producing son—to make him a star, actually auditioned for *The Monkees* TV show, thought he heard prophesies about a genocidal race war in The Beatles' lyrics on *The White Album*, and thought he was Jesus Christ."

Everything there is true—except the Monkees thing. The problem with this story is that it's simply not possible. In 1965, Manson was serving time in the penitentiary at McNeil Island in Washington state, for parole violation. He wasn't released until the spring of 1967, long after *The Monkees* was already on the air.

Chapter Six

# CYBERMYTHS AND OTHER ONLINE GOSSIP

Old-fashioned chain letters are mildly annoying, but there's something almost quaintly charming about the way they circulate around the world, compared with the annoying, staccato, rapid-fire avalanche of chain faxes and e-mails we now receive on almost a daily basis at work or home. With a few taps of the keyboard, some well-meaning friend or associate will send us yet another heavily-forwarded message warning us about some under-publicized danger, advertising a non-existent giveaway, or informing us of the latest tricky virus making the rounds.

## *Cutiegirl's dilemma*

Message to Cutiegirl: The world wants to know what you did. Did you make the right decision?

Maybe you've heard of Cutiegirl, or to be more precise, the young lady whose e-mail address is Cutiegirl52@hotmail.com. She's the star of a petition that's been making the rounds:

> Hey everyone! One of my friends is pregnant and her boyfriend won't let her have the baby. I already told him and her that it's wrong to have an abortion because you should not kill a living human being.
>
> Then I said if I could get 500 people to sign a paper that says it's wrong to have an abortion then would you let her have the baby, and he said yes. So I'm asking you please sign this petition that says having an abortion is wrong and to let her have the baby.
>
> If you are the 500th person to sign this, please send this back to Cutiegirl52@hotmail.com. Thanx.

Really now.

The amazing thing is that hundreds, if not thousands, of people have been taking this seriously for nearly two years now. They sign their names, they forward the message, they contact me and ask that I publicize Cutiegirl's plight so more people will step forward and persuade her to do the right thing and have the baby. (Of course, we don't know that having the baby is the right thing for Cutiegirl. What if she's an impoverished, 16-year-old crack addict?)

This thing has so many holes in it that it's the Swiss Cheese of Internet petitions. First of all, who is this mysterious boyfriend who "won't let" the young woman have the baby? Is he holding her hostage? Threatening to harm her if he carries to term? Doesn't sound much like daddy material to me.

And what about this supposed conversation between the person who sent the e-mail—presumably she's Cutiegirl's friend—and the young couple? Did it take place on the set of the *Jerry Springer Show*?

I sent an e-mail to Cutiegirl. It bounced back. I sent an e-mail to the person who forwarded the so-called petition to me, and *it* bounced back. You'd think that if someone were so determined to help her friend and save that unborn baby, she'd attach her name to the petition and be available for questions and comments.

Of course, there actually could be a couple of dimwits out there who are willing to decide the fate of their unborn baby based on the amount of strangers who e-mail the baby's mother. Lord knows that such attributes as intelligence and deep, careful reasoning are not prerequisites of conceiving a child. But even if there really is a person behind the Cutiegirl moniker, and that person really was pregnant, and her clown of a boyfriend really did agree to let the Internet decide the fate of the fetus, and you want to sign your name to the petition to make your feelings known, sorry, but it's too late for you to get involved. As I mentioned, the petition has been around for a few years now, which means that if Cutiegirl did decide to have the baby, it would be more than a year old by now.

Either that or Cutiegirl is 24 months pregnant, and then she'd *really* be an urban legend.

# Audrey Hepburn's beauty tips

In 1989, I went on a 12-day Caribbean cruise with the legendary and lovely Audrey Hepburn, with ports of call at the Cayman Islands, Cozumel, St. Thomas, St. Martin, and Montego Bay. During some glorious interludes, known as "at-sea days," Audrey and I never saw land at all; we just sailed the clear blue waters and enjoyed the sensuous breezes and the wonder of the moment.

I hardly noticed that 2,000 other people were with us. Well, between us, to be more accurate.

It was the inaugural voyage of the Star Princess, and Miss Hepburn (along with the equally legendary and nearly as lovely Gavin MacLeod of *Love Boat* fame) was on hand to christen the ship and to mingle with the VIPs and the travel press, of which I was a member. So I guess you could *technically* say we didn't actually go on the cruise together, but why are you quibbling with piddling details when I'm trying to tell my story of the romantic cruise I took with Audrey Golightly Hepburn!

Although her cinematic legacy includes indelible performances in movies such as *Roman Holiday*, *Sabrina*, *My Fair Lady*, and *Breakfast at Tiffany's*, Hepburn essentially retired from acting in 1980 and in her later years was much better known as a tireless humanitarian who dedicated herself to UNICEF.

In 1993, Hepburn succumbed to colon cancer, but her influence still reverberates in the world of fashion and movies, with models perennially trying to duplicate her unique style, and young actresses often citing her as their role model.

Hepburn also leaves behind an oft-quoted series of thought provoking and inspiring "Beauty Tips," which are in constant rotation on the Internet and have been quoted in a number of newspaper articles and columns. When I mentioned "Audrey Hepburn's Beauty Tips" to a friend who writes entertainment articles for the Internet, she said, "I get that e-mail about once a week."

If you haven't come across these pearls of wisdom, here's an excerpt:

> *For attractive lips, speak words of kindness*
>
> *For lovely eyes, seek out the good in people*
>
> *For a slim figure, share your food with the hungry*
>
> *For beautiful hair, let a child run his or her fingers through it once a day*
>
> *For poise, walk with the knowledge that you'll never walk alone*
>
> *People, even more than things, have to be restored, renewed, revived, reclaimed, and redeemed; never throw out anybody*
>
> *The beauty of a woman is not in the clothes she wears, the figure that she carries, or the way she combs her hair. The beauty of a woman must be seen from in her eyes, because that is the doorway to her heart, the place where love resides.*
>
> *The beauty of a woman grows with the passing years.*

These words and thoughts certainly would seem to fit the philosophy of life as Hepburn lived it; and in fact she did recite those lines on many an occasion.

But she didn't write them. Nor did she ever claim to have written them.

In fact, Hepburn—being Audrey Hepburn and not some hack actress who would try to appropriate somebody else's work as her own—always prefaced her remarks by saying the prose poem had been written by humorist Sam Levinson.

Still, one could see how some folks who heard the speech over the years would forget the mention of Levinson and quote the lines as Hepburn's, just as fans of Frank Sinatra quote "his" lyrics to this day when they're really quoting Cole Porter or Sammy Cahn. With the advent of the Internet, it was only a matter of time before Levinson's piece was reborn as "Audrey Hepburn's Beauty Tips." And with both the performer and the author gone (Levinson died in 1980), there's no one around to set the record straight.

Other than the Urban Legend Home Office, that is.

# *The virtual death of*
# *Kaycee Nicole*

Kaycee Nicole is 19 years old, a serious basketball player, and cooler than any of us will ever be.
—Internet posting by "Terri" on March 5, 2001.

By the thousands, the virtual community embraced Kaycee Nicole Swenson. Reached out to her, protected her, comforted her, prayed for her.

Loved her.

They were Kaycee's support group. It didn't matter that none of them had ever met her and that few of them had even spoken on the phone with her. She was like family, and the feelings they had for her were not cyber-pseudo emotions—they were real, honest emotions.

And she broke their hearts.

Kaycee's journey to Web celebritydom began in the spring of 2000, when she "met" a Canadian-born, Hong Kong-based writer named Randall van der Woning in cyberspace and struck up an IM, or Instant Messaging, friendship with him. (The Instant Messaging feature allows individuals to converse to each other in almost "real time," with the messages popping up on your screen mere seconds after you've hit the Send key.) Kaycee, a blonde, effervescent, high school basketball star and homecoming queen in a small town in Kansas, told van der Woning she had leukemia but was in remission.

A few months later, Kaycee informed van der Woning that the cancer had returned. He volunteered to pay for and maintain an Internet diary, known as a Weblog, for her, with photos, songs, poems, and journal entries.

"On Aug. 2 [2000], she sent me a long paper she had written titled 'Living Colours,'" van der Woning explained in a long Internet posting that ran in May 2001. "In it she detailed her story...her childhood...her experiences with loss of friends through death...even a diary of her first round with cancer."

Kaycee's first entry was indicative of her spirit:

I'm beginning an exciting new journey. It's a journey into my survival. I want to win! I'll fight to the finish!

Often Kaycee's writing was dramatic and effective, in an extended Hallmark greeting card style. In the following entry she anticipated her release from the hospital.

I stood by the window this morning. My little piece of sunlight inched its way into the room. Just a sliver of promise touching my cheek. I stood there but didn't feel alone. It was like a million smiles were shining on me, and I wasn't afraid. I wasn't ever alone...

Through the gleaming whiteness I peered into the crystal pathways of time, and the journey that brought me to this place. I didn't try to stop the tears that slowly made their way out of the corners of my eyes. They hold so many stories of trials, triumphs, happiness, frustration, agony, elation, fear, sadness, and most of all, love.

I know what a miracle is. I know love carried me all the way.

By the time Kaycee wrote those words, she had become a cult favorite on the Internet, attracting thousands of visitors to her site and inspiring tributes from fans around the world, who would often quote her words in their own Weblogs. As for van der Woning, he was the window to Kaycee's world, communicating with her almost daily, either via Instant Messages or on the telephone. He also forged a bond with Kaycee's mother, Debbie, who established a Weblog of her own.

A *New York Times* article reported that during one of Kaycee's bad spells, Debbie wrote, "I told her I loved her and everything was going to be all right. She was told not to talk or move around. Green, glassy eyes looked at me as blood trickled out of her mouth. The urge to hold her as I had when she was a child was fierce."

Some folks sent Kaycee small presents or notes to cheer her up. When she wrote about losing her hair due to the chemotherapy treatments, baseball caps and other hats arrived from all over the world.

Many said they were praying for Kaycee every day.

But she was getting worse. By the fall of 2000, Kaycee and her mother were "practically living in the hospital," according to van der Woning, who was still regularly conversing with Kaycee, who had brought a laptop computer to the hospital. They also spoke on the phone.

"On Oct. 21, Kaycee [messaged me], but she was talking gibberish," wrote van der Woning. "The things she said made no sense. After several minutes of [me] trying to convince her to ring for the nurse, Debbie took over the conversation, saying that the doctors were there. Later, she told me Kaycee's calcium levels dropped to dangerously low levels, and that somehow I had probably saved her life by telling her to send for help. I felt fortunate I was in the right place at the right time."

Through the winter and the spring, Kaycee battled through a number of setbacks while her online friends absorbed her every word and communicated their love for her. She managed to survive a number of close calls—but on May 15, van der Woning received the phone call he'd been dreading for months.

It was Debbie, sobbing hysterically. Kaycee was dead.

Randall van der Woning was as devastated as he'd been when his own father died of cancer. Yet he found the strength to comfort Debbie through a marathon grieving session on the phone that lasted three hours, and he mustered the courage to log on and inform Kaycee's support group that she was gone.

Kaycee's Weblog for that day contained an image of a rose, and the announcement: "Thank you for the love, the joy, the laughter, and the tears. We shall love you always and forever."

The virtual support group mourned their friend. She had become their heroine, their inspiration, and their beacon of hope—and now she was gone at the age of 19. Life was cruel.

Even more cruel than they first thought, actually. It turned out that Kaycee Nicole Swenson wasn't dead at all—because she had never existed.

In a cyber-twist worthy of Agatha Christie, it was an ad hoc group of Kaycee's virtual friends who uncovered one of the most elaborate hoaxes in Internet history. Within a day of Kaycee's death, some of her online friends contacted Debbie about traveling to Kansas to attend services for Kaycee, but they were informed that a service had already taken place and her body had been cremated, and that there was no address to send flowers or cards. Even more curious was the fact that there was no mention of Kaycee's death in the Obituaries of the Kansas newspapers, let alone the news sections.

The online sleuthing was on. Members of Kaycee's support group contacted one another and came to the realization that none of them had ever met her in person. One amateur detective noted that Kaycee and Debbie wrote in a similar style, including duplicate spelling errors. Another found it interesting that Kaycee always quoted lyrics from old pop songs from the 1960s and 1970s, never anything from her own generation.

Three days after Kaycee had supposedly died, she logged on to one of her accounts. A day after that, Debbie Swenson called van der Woning and explained that Kaycee's real name was Katherine Marie and that she was actually her niece, not her daughter. Swenson claimed that her sister didn't want the child, and that Kaycee had been brought up believing Swenson was her mother.

But by then the evidence was mounting that Kaycee Nicole Swenson was purely fictitious, and on May 20, Swenson confessed that the whole thing was a hoax.

It was Swenson herself who had posed as Kaycee—and as Kaycee's mother. The photos on the Weblog chronicled the life of one Julie Fullbright, a college student who lived near Swenson. Julie's mother had innocently provided Swenson with the pictures because Swenson had said she wanted to make a scrapbook of Julie's academic and athletic achievements and post it on the Web. Fullbright knew nothing about the Kaycee Nicole phenomenon until after the hoax was exposed.

(My own theory about the rather unusual name of "Kaycee Nicole" is that for some morbid reason, Swenson named her fictitious daughter after two of the victims in the school shootings in Paducah, Ken.)

The FBI was contacted, but because the gifts sent to "Kaycee" amounted to only a few hundred dollars, they declined to press charges. "The loss isn't great enough for the FBI to open up a federal criminal investigation," an FBI spokesman told the *New York Times*.

As for Randall van der Woning, by all accounts he was nothing but a well-meaning dupe. After Swenson's ruse was exposed, van der Woning wrote an anguished, six-page chronicle of his experiences, titled, "The End of the Whole Mess." He also removed any and all references to Kaycee from his archives.

"I hope my story will help people understand what happened, and, perhaps, if I'm fortunate, it will help us all learn to trust each other again," he wrote. "I won't stop caring about people. I'm not going to change who I am. I like me. I have a life to live. Time to go live it."

Good advice. In retrospect, it's easy to say that van der Woning and others should have been more suspicious and more cautious from the start. Why was a grown man striking up a friendship with a teenage girl on the Internet anyway? Why did Kaycee always dodge people when they said they wanted to visit her in person?

For that matter, Debbie/Kaycee must have always been the one who made the phone calls. A simple call to a hospital would have revealed that there was no patient named Kaycee Nicole Swenson registered.

Swenson told the media she didn't feel bad about her deeply disturbing behavior, because the invention of Kaycee led to such an outpouring of genuine affection. In her own sick mind, she thinks she accomplished something good.

Wrong. Her actions might not fit the legal definition of a crime, but what she did was much worse than conning people out of money.

She hijacked their sorrow.

# *"The Paradox of Our Time"*

Cyber clutter is the bane of our computer lives. If you could magically eliminate all the unsolicited sales pitches, corny jokes, forwarded virus warnings, community announcements, and cc'd group messages from your e-mailbox, you'd probably reduce your intake by 50 percent or more. The only difference between junk e-mail and junk snail mail is that you click "delete" for the former and crumple up the latter.

When I'm sifting through my inbox I feel like a 21st century version of the 1840s dreamers who panned for treasure during the Gold Rush. You have to fight your way through a lot of dust and worthless rocks and fool's gold to find the occasional gleaming nugget that comes in the form of a heartfelt e-letter from a long-lost friend or even a poignant mass e-mailing that touches your heart.

For example, "The Paradox of Our Time."

Perhaps you've been on the receiving end of this thoughtful essay, which has been reprinted in newspaper articles, read on the air by radio hosts and even quoted at length in sermons. It goes something like this:

## The Paradox of Our Time

*The paradox of our time in history is that we have taller buildings, but shorter tempers; wider freeways, but narrower viewpoints.*

*We spend more, but have less; we buy more, but enjoy it less.*

*We have bigger houses and smaller families; more conveniences, but less time.*

*We have more degrees, but less sense; more knowledge, but less judgment; more experts, but more problems, more medicine, but less wellness.*

*We drink too much, smoke too much, spend too recklessly, laugh too little, drive too fast, get too angry too quickly, stay up too late, get up too tired, read too seldom, watch TV too much, and pray too seldom.*

*We have multiplied our possessions, but reduced our values.*

*We talk too much, love too seldom, and hate too often.*

*We've learned how to make a living, but not a life; we've added years to life, not life to years.*

*We've been all the way to the moon and back, but have trouble crossing the street to meet a new neighbor.*

*We've conquered outer space, but not inner space.*

*We've done larger things, but not better things.*

*We've cleaned up the air, but polluted the soul.*

*We've split the atom, but not our prejudice.*

*We write more, but learn less.*

*We plan more, but accomplish less.*

*We've learned to rush, but not to wait…*

*These are days of quick trips, disposable diapers, throwaway morality, one-night stands, overweight bodies, and pills that do everything from cheer to quiet to kill.*

*It is a time when there is much in the show window*

*and nothing in the stockroom; a time when technology can bring this letter to you, and a time when you can choose either to share this insight, or just hit delete.*

Quite a snack for thought! And if the words aren't enough to give you pause, know this: the author of "The Paradox of Our Time" was a high school student—at Columbine. His family found the essay on the hard drive of his PC, and they posted it on the Internet so the world could hear the boy's voice after he had been tragically silenced.

Now, if you actually believe that, I want you to go back to the beginning of the book and start reading again, because you've obviously been distracted.

Of course a Columbine student didn't write this thing. That would happen only if Hallmark and O. Henry had created the world. The real author of the piece is an online scribe named Jeff Dickson, who posted it on the Hacks-R-Us site in the spring of 1998, and quickly saw it take flight from his possession and soar into cyberspace—much like the cases of Mary Schmich's infamous "Wear Sunscreen" column for the *Chicago Tribune*, which morphed into a Kurt Vonnegut commencement address, or an old humor column by yours truly that for years has been attributed to *Simpsons* creator Matt Groening. (See my book *Hollywood Urban Legends* for the full story.)

While giving Dickson full credit for penning this simplistic but admittedly intriguing essay, I can't help but take issue with some of the arguments he forwards, e.g., "We have...more medicine, but less wellness." In what sense? A hundred years ago, the average American was fortunate to live past 50; today, you've got a reasonable shot at hitting 80 or even 90. And if Dickson is referring to "wellness" in the psychological or spiritual sense, well, never before have there been so many treatments and options for those seeking therapy or religious solace.

I also take issue with the claim that "we've split the atom, but not our prejudice." Certainly it's true that racial and ethnic hatred continues to plague societies the world over—but could anyone make the argument that we're collectively *less* tolerant and enlightened than we were before the Civil Rights movement, before the fall of the Berlin Wall, before the end of apartheid in South Africa? Come on.

"The Paradox of Our Time" falls into the common trap of bemoaning the current state of life while falsely believing that past generations somehow had a better grasp of the true value of life, but if we could travel back in time, my hunch is we'd learn that everyone thinks his or her era is more complicated than the one before.

Life is simpler only in the rearview mirror.

Another widely circulated e-mail cites the words of Darrell Scott, father of slain Columbine student Rachel Scott, in a speech to Congress in May 1999. Excerpts from Scott's address are usually preceded by an emotional plea that "every parent, every teacher, every politician, should read this!"

Scott's speech included a poem with this stanza:

> *Your laws ignore our deepest needs*
> *Your words are empty air*
> *You've stripped away our heritage*
> *You've outlawed simple prayer!*

Scott went on to say, "To those of you who would point your finger at the NRA, I give to you a sincere challenge. Dare to examine your own heart before casting the first stone! My daughter's death will not be in vain! The young people of this country will not allow that to happen!"

The e-mail version of Scott's speech often includes a coda: "Be courageous enough to do what the media did not—let the nation hear this man's speech. Please send this out to everyone you can!"

You can see why Scott's speech would be a favorite of special interest groups, e.g., the gun lobby and the prayer-in-school folks. Here we have the father of a young martyr, refusing to blame the NRA and calling for a return to God! If anyone has the right to curse the heavens and call for a universal ban on guns, it would be someone like Darrell Scott.

The fact is that Mr. Scott indeed did address Congress on May 27, 1999, and the quotes in the e-mail attributed to him are accurate. What's not accurate is the claim that the media somehow buried this story. Scott's speech was quoted in newspaper and on newscasts across the country.

From the May 28, 1999, *Seattle Post-Intelligencer*: "Darrell Scott of Littleton, Colo., told the House Judiciary Committee's subcommittee on crime that he blames the April 20 death of his daughter, Rachel Joy Scott, 17, on Eric Harris and Dylan Klebold.

"There are people behind those instruments of death," Scott told the panel. "I do believe Eric and Dylan bear primary responsibility for my daughter's death, not the guns themselves."

That same day, the *Atlanta Constitution and Journal* reported that "Darrell Scott, the father of a teenage daughter killed at Columbine High School and a son who was wounded, told lawmakers not to scapegoat the NRA and work to reintegrate God and prayer into the classroom."

Scott's appearance was also given prominent play in the *Baltimore Sun*, the *Denver Rocky Mountain News* and the *Hartford Courant*, among other papers, and was reported on by NPR,

CNN, ABC, and CBS. His appearances at rallies since then have also been given fair play to the media.

The speech itself is not urban legend—but the claim that the liberal media ignored Scott's conservative views is nonsense.

# *Nike shoe rebate*

Most old gym shoes are nothing more than smelly fodder for the dumpster, but some well-worn Nike relics are rare treasures worth big bucks on the open market. If you've got an original pair of Air Jordans from the mid-1980s, for example, there are people in Japan willing to pay hundreds of dollars (or even more) to take them off your hands. This isn't an urban legend, this is a true fact from the kinky world of collectibles, a world where Mark McGwire's 70th home run ball is valued at $3 million and cookie jars once owned by Andy Warhol can sell for $1,000 or more.

Even more mundane pairs of old Nikes can serve a purpose, as the image-conscious company has figured out a way to recycle the rubber from those old shoes into material that can be turned into playground surfaces and basketball courts. Nike collects old gym shoes of all brands and makes them into a material called Nike Grind that is used for "new playgrounds, tennis courts, basketball courts, and running tracks," according to Nike's web site.

This recycling program undoubtedly was the root of the Internet urban legend about a "rebate" offer from Nike that seemed too good to be true. A typical E-mail:

> Just a quick note to tell you about a program that
> Nike started to help make fields and programs for the

underprivileged from old tennis shoes. All YOU have to do is send in your old tennis shoes (NO MATTER WHAT THEY LOOK LIKE) with a piece of paper that has your name and address on it, and Nike will send you a brand new pair FREE OF COST!!!!* The tennis shoes you send DO NOT have to be Nike, just as long as they are tennis shoes. It really is a worthwhile project, and it's helping a lot of young kids.

Here is the address:
Nike Recycling Center
c/o Reuse a Shoe
26755 SW 95th Street
Wilsonville, OR 97070

Otherwise you are just going to throw them out and they go to waste. This way someone can get some use out of them. Nike really does send you a BRAND NEW pair of shoes even if you send in K-Swiss. Pass this to anyone and everyone you know so everyone can help out.

You'll notice a pattern in the texts of these e-mail chain letters—they almost always read as if penned by junior high students who are attempting to imitate adults, e.g.,"Otherwise you are just going to throw them out and they go to waste." You'd think someone would elevate the grammar and clean up the syntax as the e-mail gets passed from computer to computer, but there seems to be an unwritten law of etiquette that says the original message should not be touched as it's passed along. I've received chain letters with 50 names attached, and not one person altered the "important message" in any way, not even to correct a misspelling.

Like most companies plagued by Internet hoaxes, Nike decided it was better to address the issue than to ignore it and hope it would fade away. Under the typically immodest headline, "NIKE EXPOSES INTERNET HOAX," the company released a statement that read, in part:

> BEAVERTON, OR—Internet users who are receiving and responding to e-mail messages purportedly from Nike are the unwitting victims of a hoax. Several variations are being spread across cyberspace, all claiming offers that seem too good to be true. They aren't.

"Nike never sends unsolicited e-mails over the Internet," said Scott Reames, Nike Corp. communications director. "We do not condone these e-mail hoaxes, and are dismayed that well-intentioned people are being duped into wasting their time."

Reames touched on something that is sure to be explored in surveys and studies for years to come—the amount of time wasted by people who spread rumors and/or respond to bogus offers on the Internet. All that irrelevant activity going on every day in this country! It has to add up to millions, if not billions, of dollars in lost production.

"If Nike were to make any sort of offer to consumers over the Internet, it would not be via unsolicited chain e-mails," said the company's press release.

**UL Advice:** If you receive an e-mail with more than three exclamation points at the end of a sentence, you can be almost 100 percent sure you're dealing with a hoax.

# *Blacks losing the right to vote*

The first time I heard of this disturbing urban legend was when I got a call from an African-American reader in the summer of 1998.

"Did you know blacks are going to lose the right to vote in the year 2007?" he said.

"That's crazy," I said. "What are you talking about?"

"You've got to look into this and write about it," he said. "You've got to get the word out! Remember when Lyndon Johnson signed the Voting Rights Act in the 1960s?"

"I don't remember it because I was about five at the time," I said, "but I know what you're talking about."

"Well, the key word is 'act.' I got an e-mail today explaining that the Johnson legislation was an act, not an amendment. Reagan signed a 25-year extension of the Voting Rights Act in 1982, but that expires in 2007, and blacks will no longer have the right to vote unless somebody does something about it now."

The story sounded ridiculous—after all, blacks had the right to vote long before Lyndon Johnson was in office—but I promised the caller I'd look into it.

Within days of that call, I received three or four e-mail affirmations of what I'd already discovered on my own—I was dealing with a burgeoning urban legend.

An edited version of the e-mail:

PLEASE PASS THIS ON TO AS MANY PEOPLE
AS YOU CAN!!!!!!

Do you know the significance of the year 2007 to Black
America? Did you know our right to vote will expire
that year? This is no joke.

The Voting Rights Act signed by Lyndon B. Johnson
was just an ACT. It was not made into LAW. In 1982
Ronald Reagan amended the Voting Rights Act for only
another 25 years. Which means that in year 2007 we
could lose the right to vote!

Blacks are the only group of people who still require
PERMISSION under the United States Constitution
to vote! In the year 2007 Congress will once again con-
vene to decide whether blacks should have the right to
vote. In order for this to be passed, 38 states will have
to approve another extension.

We must contact our elected representatives to put a
stop to this extension madness, and to urge them to
make it LAW that blacks have the right to vote. We
have come too far to let the government make us grovel
for the right to vote. Please pass this on to all black
brothers and sisters, and all our non-black brothers and
sisters who are true Americans and support equality
for EVERYONE.

We'll let the United States Department of Justice clarify
things, in excerpts from their official statement responding to
this rumor:

The Department of Justice has received numerous
inquiries concerning a rumor that has been intermit-
tently circulating around the nation for many months.

According to this rumor, the Voting Rights Act will expire in 2007, and as a result African Americans are in danger of losing the right to vote that year.

The rumor is false. The voting rights of African Americans are guaranteed by the United States Constitution and the Voting Rights Act, and those guarantees are permanent and do not expire. The 15th amendment to the Constitution [*which was ratified in 1870— author's note*] and the Voting Rights Act of 1965 prohibit racial discrimination in voting. Under the 15th amendment and the Voting Rights Act, no one may be denied the right to vote because of his or her race or color...

The basic prohibition against discrimination in voting contained in the 15th amendment and in the Voting Rights Act does not expire in 2007— in fact, it does not expire at all, it is permanent.

It is true that the some elements of Voting Rights Act will expire in 2007—but these items were never intended to be in effect forever. Unfortunately, there were special circumstances that led to the creation of the Voting Rights Act in the first place. For decades, blacks in the South had been harassed, threatened, assaulted, and otherwise prohibited from exercising their Constitutional right to vote. The civil rights movement led to the Voting Rights Act, which spelled out "special provisions containing extraordinary remedies," as the government put it, for a limited time period applying to specific areas where blacks were not allowed to vote. The act was scheduled to expire after five years, but it was extended in 1970 by Richard Nixon, in 1975 by Gerald Ford, and in 1982 by Ronald Reagan. No doubt whoever's in charge in 2007 will once again extend the legislation, if only for public relations purposes. Even if the special provisions section of the Voting Rights Act was allowed to expire, those provisions can be reinstated by court order if there's evidence of discriminatory practices in a particular region. And with or without the act, the 15th amendment guaranteeing all citizens of legal age the right to vote is permanent and binding.

Still, the rumor was so dominant on the Internet that in December of 1998, the *Associated Press* ran a story about it.

"[W]hat is distressing to so many black leaders is that so many black people would give even a second thought to [the] claim that their voting rights will expire in 2007, when certain provisions of the Voting Rights Act run out unless renewed by Congress," the story says. Rep. James Clyburn (D.-S.C.) told the AP his office was receiving "hundreds of calls" about the rumor. "It's frustrating dealing with this hoax," he said.

I'm thinking of sending out an e-mail of my own:

URGENT! Millions of people don't understand how the Constitution works! They're needlessly spreading rumors about blacks losing the right to vote!

Think anyone will fall for that?

## *Shannon's Internet lesson*

I wish I could give credit to the author of this cautionary tale, but I've never seen it attributed to anyone in any of the versions forwarded to me. There are some who claim this isn't a fable at all, that it's "based on a true story," but a search of newspaper articles in North Carolina, where this supposedly happened, yielded no stories that come close to resembling this fascinating story. In fact, the police chief in the town where this story supposedly transpired told me he's never heard anything about it.

This tale reads like something that was crafted by a creative writer for a community watchdog group's newsletter, police bulletin, or someone who pens mini-sermons for a non-denominational church. It also has the ring of one of those TV "after school specials" filled with high drama and a deep message.

In any case, this is one of the most widely disseminated legends on the Internet, presented here in a slightly truncated version.

It almost always begins with the header: "Something to think about..."

Shannon could hear the footsteps behind her as she walked toward home. The thought of being followed home made her heart beat faster. "You're being silly, no one is following you" she told herself. To be safe, she began to walk faster, but the footsteps kept up with her pace. She was afraid to look back and glad she was almost home. She saw the porch light and ran the rest of the way to her house.

Later she logged on to her computer under her screen name, ByAngel213. Checking her e-mail buddy list, she saw that her friend GoTo123 was online. She sent him an instant message.

ByAngel213: Hi! I'm glad you're on! I thought someone was following me home today. It was really weird!

GoTo123: You watch too much TV. Why would someone be following you? Don't you live in a safe neighborhood?

ByAngel213: Of course I do. I guess it was my imagination.

GoTo123: Unless you gave your name out online. You haven't done that, have you?

ByAngel123: Of course not. I'm not stupid you know.

GoTo123: Did you have a softball game after school today?

ByAngel123: Yes and we won!

GoTo123: What is your team called again?

ByAngel123: The Canton Cats. We have tiger paws on our uniforms

GoTo123: Do you pitch or what?

ByAngel123:    No, I play second base. I have to go, I have to do my homework before my parents get home at 6:30.

GoTo123:    Catch you later.

The individual with the screen name of GoTo123 decided it was time to teach Angel a lesson, one she would never forget. He went to the member menu and began to search for her profile. When it came up, he highlighted it and printed it out. He took out a pen and began to write down what he knew about Angel so far:

Name: Shannon.

Birthday: Jan. 3, 1985. Age: 13.

State where she lived: North Carolina

Hobbies: softball, chorus, skating, and going to the mall

He knew she lived in the town of Canton. He knew she stayed by herself until 6:30 every evening. He knew she played softball on Thursday afternoons and the team was named the Canton Cats. In previous online conversations, she had told him her favorite number was 7 and she attended Canton Junior High School. "She doesn't even know what she's done," he thought to himself.

Shannon didn't tell her parents about the incident on the way home from the ballpark that day. She didn't want them to make a scene and stop her from walking home alone from softball games. Parents were always overreacting.

By Thursday, Shannon had forgotten about the footsteps following her the week before. Her game was in full swing when suddenly she felt someone staring at her. It was then that the memory came back. She glanced up from her second base position to see a man watching her closely. He was leaning against the fence behind first base and smiled when she looked at him. He didn't look scary, so she quickly dismissed the fear she felt.

After the game, he sat in the bleachers while she talked to the coach. She noticed the man's smile once again as she walked past him.

He noticed the name on the back of her shirt. He knew he had found her. Quietly, he walked a safe distance behind her. He didn't want to frighten her and have to explain what he was doing.

It was only a few blocks to Shannon's home, and once he saw where she lived he quickly returned to the park to get his car. Now he had to wait. He decided to get a bite to eat until the time came to go to Shannon's house. He went to a fast food restaurant and sat there until it was time to make his move.

Shannon was in her room later that evening when she heard voices in the living room. Her father called for her. She came downstairs and there was the man from the softball game in her living room.

"Sit down," said her father. "This man is a policeman and he just told me a very interesting story."

"Do you know who I am?" the man asked Shannon.

"No," Shannon answered.

"I am your friend online, GoTo123."

Shannon was stunned. "That's impossible! GoTo is a kid my age! He's 14 and he lives in Michigan!"

The man smiled. "I know I told you all that, but it wasn't true. You see Shannon, there are people online who pretend to be kids; I was one of them. But while others do it to find kids and hurt them, I belong to a group of parents who do it to protect kids from predators. I came here to find you to teach you how dangerous it is to give out too much information to people online. You told me enough about yourself to make it easy for me to find you."

"You mean you don't live in Michigan?" Shannon said.

He laughed. "No, I live in Raleigh. It made you feel safe to think I was so far away, didn't it?"

She nodded.

"I had a friend who had a daughter like you and she had an online friend too," the man said. "Only she wasn't as lucky. The guy found her and murdered her while she was home alone. Kids are taught not to tell anyone when they are alone, yet they do it all the time when they're online. I hope you've learned a lesson from this and you won't do it again."

"I won't," Shannon promised.

"Will you tell others about this so they'll be safe?"

"It's a promise!"

That night Shannon and her mom and dad all knelt down together and prayed. They thanked God for protecting Shannon from a tragic situation.

Please send this to as many people as you can to teach them not to give any information about themselves. This world we live in today is too dangerous to give out even your age, let alone anything else. Be safe! PASS THIS ON!

Kind of like an episode of *Touched by An Angel*, isn't it? However, it might be a more dramatic touch if the cop told Shannon it was *his* little girl who was killed by an online predator.

As for the dad in the story, it would probably be a little more realistic if he punched the cop out for needlessly scaring the crap out of his daughter. In fact, most police forces in the country would probably fire or at least suspend an officer who went online and posed as a 14-year-old boy to stalk a 13-year-old girl in order to teach her a lesson.

# *April Fool's on the Internet*

Every year on April Fool's Day, at least a dozen elaborately constructed hoaxes are released on the Internet. In the Stone Age of the 1980s, when we still clung to the belief that cyberspace would be the last and greatest frontier for philosophical debate, lofty thought, and global communication, it was easy to fall for April Fool's Day pranks. Bogus press releases and phony warnings of impending computer doom were taken seriously by many of us in the media, and were often picked up by serious news organizations as legitimate stories.

Now it's almost become a sporting event. When you log on to your computer on April 1, you fully expect to be inundated with jokes, pranks, hoaxes, and scams, and you come to appreciate the more creative efforts.

There have literally been hundreds of these pranks over the last decade. The ones excerpted here are representative of the genre.

## George Lucas abandons *Star Wars*

April 1, 1997, 8:13 AM EST

Lucas Scraps *Star Wars* Prequels

By Kevin Somers

(HOLLYWOOD)—With the *Star Wars Trilogy Special Editions* still gobbling up sales receipts at the box office, some bad news has arisen from the Lucasfilm camp. George Lucas, creator of *Star Wars* and its two sequels, has retracted his promise of a second trilogy of the *Star Wars* films. Mere days ago, Lucasfilm announced plans to start principal photography on *Star Wars—Episode 1* on Sept. 8 of this year. The film was already deep into preproduction. Trouble began late last week when Lucas scrapped 70 percent of the script for the third part of the new trilogy.

When asked why he would turn down the chance to again thrill filmgoers with his sci-fi epic, as well as pass up what would invariably be a windfall in box office grosses, Lucas was quoted as saying "It just isn't going well. Casting has been difficult. We've been unable to find anyone suitable for the roles." Lucas also said that technological limitations have failed to sustain his vision of the films. "I've waited this long for [the technology] to catch up with my imagination, but we're not quite there yet." Lucas plans to return to the project eventually, "but not for a while."

The films were to take place several years before the existing trilogy. The first film of the proposed second trilogy, *Balance of the Force*, was to open in May 1999.

(Reuters/Variety)


I give four stars to this parody story. The byline, the dateline, the parenthetical paraphrasing in the bogus quotes—all nicely done, in the style of a professional journalist. The story has the feel of authenticity, and no doubt launched a million anxiety attacks among dedicated Jedi-heads.

Of course, the fourth *Star Wars* movie *The Phantom Menace* became one of the top five hits of all time.

## Bill Gates runs for president

April 1, 1996, 8:20 AM EST

BELLEVUE (CNN) — In a terse press release this morning, Bill Gates announced he would "succeed where Forbes has failed." In other words, he intends to be part of the presidential race—and win it. "I will run as an independent candidate well above out-dated quarrels opposing Democrats and Republicans," he wrote. "I will bring the Information Highway into every American Home. We are entering the era of Digital Democracy," he added.

The press release didn't mention whether he intended to resign from his current position at Microsoft. According to rumors, even though he set his company on a new course to try to tap the vast potential of the Internet, he is secretly doubting this attempt will succeed in the long run, and is now looking for new challenges, and might relinquish his position.

Bill Gates could not be reached for comment.

Uploaded 04/01/1996 — 09:17 PST

While the idea of Bill Gates running for president isn't completely preposterous, this attempt to hornswaggle people is pretty weak. Compared to the bogus *Star Wars* story, this is an amateurish attempt to imitate an actual wire service story. You wouldn't put the "succeed where Forbes has failed" quote in your lead, you'd simply say, "In one of the most stunning political announcements in recent history, Microsoft founder Bill Gates has stated his intentions to run for the presidency."

And consider this quote, supposedly said by Gates: "I will run as an independent candidate well above out-dated quarrels opposing Democrats and Republicans." Huh? One would like to think Bill Gates actually makes sense when he speaks.

Then there's the factor of timing. By April of 1996, we were already well into the primary season; it would have been a little late for Gates to make a serious run at the presidency, even with a virtually unlimited personal campaign fund.

## Postings:

➤ Mattel introduces "Hacker Barbie," the first computer rendition of the pneumatic doll. Russia joins the cyberspace race with a with an invitation for everyone to "open a flask of vodka."

➤ Shamed skater Tonya Harding writes a letter sarcastically "thanking" everyone for their support.

➤ Microsoft announces its intention to purchase the Vatican.

The wackiness on April 1 knows no bounds.

Also popular on April Fool's Day are the doomsday warnings about mysterious and deadly viruses that will "erase everything from your hard drive" if you even dare to look at the file containing the killer bug. Everything from screen savers featuring the Budweiser frogs to programs from America Online have been identified (falsely of course) as carriers of dangerous viruses. (Example: "If you receive an E-mail with message with the subject line 'Good Times,' DO NOT read the message. DELETE IT IMMEDIATELY. It has a virus that rewrites your hard drive, obliterating anything on it!") These messages are usually pretty scary because even though your instincts tell you it's not a legitimate warning, you know there are 15-year-old geniuses holed up in their bedrooms somewhere who do have the ability and the warped sense of humor to create havoc on the Internet. For that reason, I never open a file from an unknown sender, whether it's April Fool's Day or Arbor Day.

# *The PC cupholder*

Time now for a quickie urban legend devoid of any racist undertones, deeper underlying sociological meanings, false information about corporations, or bogus quotes attributed to celebrities. It's just fun.

The setup: A computer neophyte calls a technical help hotline.

**Caller:**   "The cup holder on my PC is broken."

**Technical Support Representative (TSR):**
        "The cup holder?"

**Caller:**   "You know, the cup holder attached to the front of the modem."

**TSR:**    "I'm confused. What are we talking about, some kind of freebie you were given with the computer? Is this an attachment you got at a computer trade show or something?"

**Caller:**   "No, no, no. It came with the computer. It's *part* of the computer. You push a button and it slides right out. The problem is, I slammed my chair into it and it snapped off, and I can't figure out how to reattach it. It's a shame, too, because I really liked having that cup holder there."

(A long silence.)

**TSR:**    "Um, that's not a cup holder, that's the load drawer of your CD-ROM, sir."

Chapter Seven

# TALL TALES OF THE RICH AND FAMOUS

It's amazing how many people profess to know the "inside scoop" about celebrities. Not surprisingly, these folks who have the inside dirt don't even work in the entertainment industry; heck, most of 'em have never even been to Los Angeles. Nevertheless, they "know" these things to be true.

Why do we all buy into these tales so eagerly? Maybe it's because we're so envious of those blessed few who seem to be living such charmed lives that we can't help but concoct, spread, and swallow such gossip.

I'm naming names in this section not to perpetuate these urban legends, but to shine the light of truth on them as showbiz myths. Not surprisingly, most celebs and their representatives are usually reluctant to even comment on such rumors—you don't want to dignify these stories by even acknowledging they're out there. But they are, and they're not going to fade away naturally...

# *Richard Gere and the gerbil*

In 1990, the actor Richard Gere met with members of the entertainment media in Los Angeles to promote *Internal Affairs*, a thriller about a Machiavellian cop (Gere) who does battle with a hot-tempered but dedicated internal affairs investigator played by Andy Garcia. Journalists were gathered in groups of eight per table in a large hotel suite, and Gere and other members of the cast rotated from table to table for 30-minute mini-press conferences. I was at one of those tables, and I found Gere to be a thoughtful and well-mannered person who patiently answered all questions.

The gerbil rumor was just starting to take flight then. It is one of the most enduring and more mean-spirited urban legends of our times. It is so ingrained in the pop consciousness that it seemed only natural the self-referential kids in *Scream* would make a joke about it. Of course, everyone has heard the story by now and nobody believes it's true.

You don't really think Richard Gere was once rushed to a hospital emergency room, where doctors found that a gerbil had become lodged in his rectum during a wild bout of sexual play, do you?

The UL is probably a derivation of a story I heard many times in the 1970s, involving either an anonymous disco dancer, or, in some cases, John Travolta himself, who passes out from excessive partying and is brought to an emergency room where doctors remove his ultra-tight white pants and find that the guy had taped a sausage to his inner thigh. In the both stories, the point seems to be that the macho stud king is not the man he appears to be.

Before Gere was named the "star" of the gerbil rumor, local television personalities and politicians in cities from New York to Tulsa to Kansas City were the subject of the same story. In dozens of cities, people who claimed to have sources like "a buddy of mine who is married to the best friend of the emergency room nurse," were confidently claiming that the mayor or city councilman or the guy who does the local weather had been in the hospital recently, having a furry little creature extracted from his buttocks.

The tabloid press tried for years to chase down the gerbil story, but nobody was ever able to find the least bit of concrete evidence confirming that Gere (or for that matter, anyone)has ever been "de-gerbilized" by emergency room physicians.

Why was Richard Gere singled out as the target of the gerbil story? Though Gere has lived with and been linked with a succession of fantastically beautiful women—even before he became famous—his sexuality has been the subject of coarse speculation.

Around the time *Pretty Woman* was released, an anonymously circulated fax landed in Hollywood offices and in hundreds of newsrooms. It was supposedly from an animal rights group, protesting Gere's "inhumane treatment" of gerbils—an obvious reference to the rumor that was already fairly well-known by then. Nobody ever figured out where that fax originated, but it helped fuel a fire that still burns nearly a decade later.

Gere himself has never commented directly on the rumor, but in 1991, Barbara Walters gently asked Gere about "salacious rumors." Gere stated in typical Zen fashion, "If I am a cow and someone says I'm a zebra it doesn't make me a zebra."

In a Sept. 5, 1995 piece in the *Palm Beach Post,* reporter/ editor Mike Walker of the *National Enquirer* was asked about his dogged efforts to confirm the Gere/gerbil story. Walker told the *Post* he'd been trying to nail the story for years but was convinced it was completely without merit.

## *Mariah Carey's callous remark*

A lot of people seem to resent Mariah Carey. They apparently feel she's been just too darn lucky in life, and needs to be put in her place. If only the world knew what an uncaring and self-centered person she really is! Take for example what happened in the summer of 1996. Carey gave an interview where she talked about her struggles to say thin. "When I watch TV and see those poor starving kids all over the world, I can't help but cry. I mean, I'd love to be skinny like that, but not with all those flies and death and stuff."

Can you believe she'd say something like that? Only somebody who's lived a sheltered life filled with adoring fans and untold riches could look at broadcasts of starving children and envy their physiques!

Had Carey issued such a remark, she'd deserve to be flogged for it. But she didn't. Carey never said anything even close to that, but the quote has dogged the singing superstar for years. It first appeared in an interview published on the Internet—a parody interview concocted by a mischievous prankster writing for the *Cupcake* Web site. That was harmless enough, but the quote was picked up by several legitimate publications, including the British newspaper *The Independent*, the *San Francisco Chronicle* and *Ms.* Magazine. (By this point the fictitious Web site interview had given way to a supposed radio interview Carey had given.) One Internet scholar/philosopher posted the quote and then launched into a two-page essay about the greater meaning of such a remark. "Statements like Ms. Carey's often make one wonder if human nature is so inescapably flawed that eventually the species will forget how to breathe."

Relax. She never said it. There's hope yet for humanity!

By the fall of 1996, the quote was being denied by Carey's publicist—Carey herself denied it in a press conference in London—but the line was still floating out there as a legitimate comment, often appearing in those little boxes in newspapers and magazines where they feature notable quotes from celebrities. Never a favorite with the critics or sophisticated music fans, Carey was an easy target for editors and writers who *wanted* the quote to be real. Who cares if she does charity work and benefit concerts? Why bother to contact her representatives to find out if she really said such a horrendous thing about starving children? Better to run with the quote and let readers howl at the insensitivity of the rich and famous star.

Shortly after the "starving kids" rumor appeared to finally be dying down, Carey was victimized by another bogus quote. After King Hussein of Jordan died in February of 1999, the following post appeared on the Internet:

*USA Today*, Monday, Feb. 8, 1999
Mariah Carey was one of the first celebrities to comment on the death of the king of Jordan. Mariah told CNN, "I'm inconsolable at the present time. I was a very good friend of Jordan, he was probably the greatest basketball player this country has ever seen. We will never see his like again."

When told by reporters it was King Hussein of Jordan who had died and not Michael Jordan, Mariah was then led away by security in a state of confusion.

Once again, we're invited to believe the pop star is an out-and-out nincompoop with a first-grader's comprehension of world events. Of course, Carey offered no such quote to CNN, and *USA Today* featured no such item.

**UL Footnote:** In 2001, Carey's real-life behavior eclipsed any rumors about her. In May, she got into a hair-pulling wrestling match with co-star Mira Sorvino on the set of their film "Wise Girls." Over the summer, Carey posted and recorded a series of increasingly bizarre messages on her fan site, rambling on about her cat, her management company, and how she was "in a bad place." After a bizarre appearance on MTV's "Total Request Live," in which she handed out ice cream treats and stripped to reveal a skimpy bra top, and a promotional stop at a mall in which she was so incoherent her publicist snatched the microphone away, Carey checked herself into a hospital for "exhaustion." Later her publicist confirmed that the singer had suffered an emotional breakdown, but she denied reports of drug abuse and suicide attempts.

# The misunderstanding on the elevator

For more than 20 years, a black celebrity has been getting on an elevator and uttering a command that is misinterpreted by a frightened white woman, who always reacts to the command in the same way. First the celebrity was Bill Cosby; then it was Richard Pryor, then it was Lionel Ritchie. Sports figures Mike Tyson, Magic Johnson, Wilt Chamberlain, Dennis Rodman, O.J. Simpson, Mean Joe Greene and Shaquille O'Neal have also been on the elevator. In later versions it was Eddie Murphy, and in 1999 I heard it was Sean "Puffy" Combs.

Sometimes the elevator misunderstanding takes place in New York, other times it's in Las Vegas. But while the celebrity and the locale change from telling to telling, the story remains essentially the same.

We'll go with a version starring Eddie Murphy in New York.

Two middle-aged white women from the Midwest come to New York for a business convention. They're in the elevator of a hotel in Manhattan, heading down to the lobby, when it stops on the 12th floor for an entourage consisting of three very intimidating-looking black men, all dressed in leather and gold chains, and a growling Doberman who bares its teeth at the women.

"Sit!" commands one of the men—and the women immediately obey, sitting on the floor of the elevator.

"No, I meant the dog!" says the man, who apologizes to the women and helps them to their feet, as his companions try to stifle their laughter. The women nervously laugh off the incident and explain to the man that they've never been to New York before. In an effort to downplay what just happened, they make idle, awkward conversation, with the women asking the celebrity if perhaps he can recommend a good restaurant. He does just that, and the two groups part company in the lobby.

Later that evening, the two women have a lovely meal at the restaurant recommended by the man from the elevator. When they ask the waiter for the check, he explains that it's already been taken care of, courtesy of Eddie Murphy, the famous comedian and actor.

One of the women says, "But why would Eddie Murphy pay for our dinner? We don't know him, and he certainly doesn't know us."

And then it dawns on her. Murphy was the man on the elevator, the one who issued the command to "Sit." Still feeling bad about the misunderstanding, he had arranged to pick up the check. What a guy!

In a variation, the incident takes place in Las Vegas and a white woman is so flustered by the "Sit!" confusion that when the elevator doors open, she dashes out of the elevator and doesn't even realize she has dropped her gambling chips or (in some tellings) her bucket of coins. The next morning, Room Service brings her the winnings, plus a $100 chip and a note from the celebrity, thanking her for the best laugh he's had in a long time and wishing her good luck at the tables.

Unlike other racially motivated urban legends that prey on stereotypes without offering any sort of a lesson, this one does contain some positive elements. If anything, it's an indictment of the irrational fears of some white people, as the supposedly threatening black gentleman is not only a harmless fellow, he's an accomplished and famous man who feels so bad about the women's embarrassment that *he* apologizes to *them*, when it should be the other way around. He's so generous he even arranges to pay for their dinner. If you're Murphy or any of the other prominent figures who have been named as the man in the elevator, you'd have to say it's a lot better than, say, Richard Gere's urban legend!

In the early 1980s, when I first heard the story, baseball great Reggie Jackson was supposedly the guy on the elevator, and columnists at a number of newspapers (including the *Cincinnati Enquirer* and the *Detroit Free Press* ) were reporting the incident as fact—or at least something they believed could be true, based on their reliable sources. Jackson and his agent issued a number of denials, but it did little to stop the story from spreading.

**UL Footnote:** It's possible this UL has its origins in an episode of the old "Bob Newhart Show," the one in which Newhart played a psychiatrist, as the source for this story. In the episode, one of Bob's patients is a large black man with a black Great Dane named Whitey; after his session with Dr. Hartley, the black man goes into the lobby, where Jerry the dentist is hanging out. The man says, "Sit, Whitey!"—whereupon Jerry perches on Carol the receptionist's desk.

# *Tiger Woods at the strip club*

When Tiger Woods roared onto the scene a few years ago, the hype was overwhelming. After Woods was named *Sports Illustrated's* "Sportsmen of the Year" in 1996 and won the Masters in 1997, the expectations were raised to the level of the absurdly unrealistic. He was featured in a series of Nike ads, was mobbed by crowds who treated him like a rock star, and appeared on the covers of magazines, from *GQ* to *SI* as frequently as Michael Jordan.

Tiger's fame was such that he was accorded perhaps the ultimate celebrity status symbol in late 1996 and early 1997—his very own urban legend, told to this day as a true anecdote on sports talk shows and in barroom conversation.

Here's how it was told to me:

In 1996, when Woods was just 20 and in Las Vegas for a tournament, he and a group of friends decided to check out one of the infamous strip joints in town. All of Tiger's buddies were waved in, but the surly bouncer put a meaty paw on the young golfer's chest, regarded Tiger's youthful visage, and demanded identification. Tiger figured that his celebrity status would gain him immediate entrance, so he confidently took out his driver's license and handed it to the bouncer, who shined a flashlight on it and frowned.

"Says here you're only 20, Mr. Woods," he said. "Sorry, pal, you've got to be 21 to see what goes on in here."

"But I'm the Tiger!" exclaimed the golfing superstar.

"Hey, I don't care if you're the lion or the bear, you're not getting in," the bouncer replied.

The Oct. 28 sports section of the *Chicago Tribune* referred to a "Milwaukee paper's" report about Woods playing in the Quad-City Classic tournament and trying to get into an area bar, only to be thwarted by a bouncer who carded him.

"Woods: 'I don't need an I.D. I'm the Tiger.'

"Bouncer: 'I don't care if you're the Lion King. You ain't getting in here unless you have an I.D.' "

What are the odds that two bouncers in two different locales would use similar lines to turn back such a beloved celebrity?

I dug up that "Milwaukee paper" account, which the *Tribune* had quoted accurately. It originally appeared in a sports notebook column in the Oct. 20, 1996 edition of the *Milwaukee Journal Sentinel*, with the caveat that the incident was "said to have taken place at the American Bar, a popular joint in the Quad Cities area."

Let's get real here. Even when Woods was 20, he would have had no trouble gaining entrance into any club or bar in the world. What tavern owner or strip club operator wouldn't love to have a picture on his wall of Tiger Woods whooping it up in his joint?

# *Tommy Hilfiger unfairly maligned*

A few years ago, a colleague of mine (who is black) told me she would never let her two sons wear anything designed by Tommy Hilfiger, "because of what he said on Oprah's show." Her strong but misguided stance proves once again that urban legends die hard.

A typical version of the story:

Did you see designer Tommy Hilfiger's recent appearance on the *Oprah Winfrey Show*? He said that if he had known so many blacks and Chinamen were going to buy his clothes, he wouldn't have made them so nice. "I wish those people would not buy my clothes," he told Oprah. "They were made for up-per-class whites." To her credit, Oprah threw him off the show and advised her viewers to burn any Tommy Hilfiger clothes they might have in their possession. She also suggested that everyone boycott Tommy Hilfiger. What a great idea. That'll teach him a lesson about his racist ways.

The facts:

➢   Hilfiger is so popular with black rappers that he has been immortalized in hip-hop songs.

> ➤ A large percentage of Hilfiger's customers are minorities.

> ➤ The chairman of Hilfiger's company is Asian-American.

> ➤ Hilfiger told the *Los Angeles Times*, in 1996, "I'm complimented [that many rappers wear my clothes]. I know they can wear anything, yet they choose my clothes. It is a true, true honor. I think these kids are so cool."

> ➤ Hilfiger never made the cavalierly racist remarks. In fact, he's never even been a guest on *Oprah*.

Nevertheless, the remark was getting so much play on the rumor circuit that the company issued an official denial, which read in part:

> Tommy Hilfiger did not make the alleged inappropriate racial comments...Hilfiger wants his clothing to be enjoyed by people of all backgrounds and his collections are put together with the broadest cross-section of individuals in mind. To reinforce this, he features models of all ethnic backgrounds on his fashion shows and advertisements.

On Jan. 11, 1999, Winfrey took the extraordinary step of addressing the UL at the beginning of her program.

"I just wanted to set the record straight once and for all," she said. "The rumor claims that clothing designer Tommy Hilfiger came on this show and made racist remarks, and that I kicked him out. I want to say this is not true because it just never happened. Tommy Hilfiger has never appeared on this show. Read my lips: Tommy Hilfiger has never appeared on this show! It never happened. I've never even met Tommy Hilfiger."

Unfortunately, even a straightforward denial like that will never totally kill the rumor. To this day there are people who *swear* they saw the show in which Oprah kicked Hilfiger off the stage.

Hilfiger has been dogged by that rumor for years—but Liz Claiborne has been fighting a similar rumor for the better part of an entire decade. (In fact the Hilfiger legend is probably a spinoff of the Claiborne myth.) First, Claiborne was accused of uttering racist remarks to CNN's fashion reporter Elsa Klensch; then it was reported that she was a guest on *Oprah* when she made the unforgivable comments.

"Don't buy Liz Claiborne clothes!" began one fax I received a couple of years ago. "Liz Claiborne is a racist, and she showed her true nature on a recent episode of the *Oprah Winfrey Show*. Oprah wore a Liz Claiborne gown and had Claiborne on as a favor to promote Claiborne's clothing, but Claiborne turned on her during the broadcast when she said, 'My clothes were not designed for black women.'

"When Oprah asked her what she meant by that, Claiborne elaborated: 'My clothes are not designed for black women, Oprah, because black women's hips are too big and they look horrible in my clothes.' A gasp went through the crowd, but everyone cheered when Oprah threw Claiborne off the set. When they came back from the commercial, Oprah was in a bathrobe, and with tears in her eyes she urged everyone to boycott Claiborne, who had told Oprah during the break that she supported the KKK!"

You'll recall the *Oprah Winfrey Show* was also mentioned as the program on which a psychic predicted a massacre on a college campus. Before Oprah took over as the queen of daytime television, *Donahue* was often cited as the show on which some remarkable incident or comment took place. To source a specific program, especially one with such credibility as Oprah's, is no accident; it gives the rumor a certain veracity that it wouldn't have if, say, *Springer* was mentioned. Hearing that it happened on *Oprah* means it must be true. For years, publicists for Oprah's program have patiently told reporters and irate fans not to worry—none of these alleged incidents ever occurred.

In 1997, a new bastardization of the rumor surfaced. This time it was the popular hip-hop singer Lauryn Hill who had appeared on *Oprah* or some other show, stunning the audience of mostly middle-aged, suburban housewives by declaring, "I'd rather kill my baby than have white people listening to my music." A caller to Howard Stern's show claimed he'd heard her make the remarks on MTV. Not true.

# *Keanu Reeves marries David Geffen*

Rumors about a wedding between actor Keanu Reeves and media mogul David Geffen crested in late 1995 and early 1996, as media circles swirled with off-the-record but increasingly loud whispers about a ceremony at Malibu or Mexico, with Geffen and Reeves exchanging vows in front of a small gathering of their closest friends. Afterward Geffen supposedly took Reeves on a "honeymoon shopping spree" at noted clothier, Barney's, where the actor ran up thousands of dollars in charges. Reeves has been linked with many women, but he played a bisexual hustler in *My Own Private Idaho*, which unfortunately provides enough fodder for the rumor mill to start churning.

Geffen reacted to the wedding story with good humor. He also opined that the rumor most likely wasn't started by gays looking to make Reeves one of their own (for lack of a better term), but by someone wishing to hurt Reeves—perhaps even a woman looking to get even with him.

"I think these stories reflect frustration on the part of some women who simply do not get the response they want from these men," Geffen told *Vanity Fair*. "It could be that the men are not interested, or they may be involved with someone else, but it's easier to label them as gay."

The truth was that at the time the rumor was in heavy rotation on the urban legend play list, Geffen hadn't even met Reeves, let alone embarked on a whirlwind romance culminating in an oceanside marriage ceremony.

In a 1995 profile, *Out* magazine was the first publication to directly question Reeves about the supposed wedding, and he of course denied it (while also saying, "That's cool, that's cool," when told many gay men find him attractive). "Oh, yes!" he told the magazine when asked about the rumors. "I first heard it when I was in Winnepeg, on my answering machine. My friend Claire called and said, 'I heard you got married, congratulations.'"

"I guess I should return the clothes," Reeves said jokingly. But he added: "I didn't really think about [the rumor] much."

Reeves also told *Vanity Fair* the story wasn't true, but he refused to state his sexual orientation for the record: "There's nothing wrong with being gay," he said, "so to deny it is to make a judgment. And why make a big deal out of it?"

# *Newman's cone*

Even the most jaded types find themselves acting differently when in the presence of a celebrity. If you're in a restaurant or at a ballgame and a famous person happens to be seated nearby, you can try all you want to be cool and blasé about the whole thing, but you're very aware that you're doing it.

Many people don't even try to play it cool when they see a celebrity, even if it's someone whose work they don't particularly appreciate. I've seen perfectly rational, mature adults turn into raving idiots just because a mid-level rock star or an actor from a popular sitcom has entered a room. In my adventures as an entertainment journalist, I saw the crazed look in people's eyes when they realized they were coming face to face with a major celebrity.

This is not to say I think I'm above such silly but usually harmless starstruck behavior. I was a jaded, 30-year-old reporter who had met hundreds of celebrities when I was introduced to Paul Newman, and I managed to maintain an outward appearance of calm as I said, "How ya doin' Paul, I'm Richard Roeper from Chicago," but inside there was a little man running through the corridors of my brain, hollering, "We're meeting Cool Hand Luke, Butch Cassidy, and Fast Eddie Felson! Yeah!"

Imagine being Paul Newman and knowing that every time you meet someone, they're thinking something like that. It must be extremely flattering and extremely exhausting. Paul Newman never gets a day off from being Paul Newman—not even when he's waiting in line at an ice cream shop on Main Street in a little town called Urban Legendville, USA.

Actually the shop was located in Massachusetts, or in the Hamptons, or in Connecticut, as the story goes. A crabby old gal was in line at the town's quaint ice cream shop, muttering under her breath about the slow service. "These kids today are so lazy," she said. "Lazy and just plain stupid!"

"Ah, they're not so bad," says a gravelly voice behind her.

She turned to give the man a piece of her mind—and that's when she found herself looking right into the famous blue eyes of Paul Newman, her all-time favorite movie star! For one of the few times in her life, the woman was reduced to a babbling, nearly incoherent fool as she prattled on to the smiling Newman about everything and anything.

She was still in a daze as she paid for her ice cream cone and walked to her car, shaking with excitement from the experience.

Only when she put the key in the ignition did the woman come to the realization that she didn't have her ice cream cone. She exited the car, hurried back into the shop, marched past everyone who was waiting in line, and berated the young cashier for his stupidity and dishonesty.

The startled cashier said, "But I gave you—"

"Don't interrupt me!" said the lady. "That's the trouble with you young people, you're always interrupting your elders and—"

The woman was interrupted again, this time by a tap on her shoulder. She wheeled around with fire in her eyes, but her anger subsided when she saw that it was none other than Mr. Newman, who had been trying to enjoy his caramel sundae as she began her tirade.

"Don't take it out on the boy," Newman said. "He gave you the ice cream cone, dear. You put it in your pocketbook."

This story was all the rage in the mid-1980s. Usually Paul Newman was the celebrity, but in other instances it was Tom Brokaw, Dan Rather, Robert Redford, or Jack Nicholson. None of them has ever experienced anything like the ice cream cone incident in real life, though Nicholson once did tell his limo driver to make a diversion to a liquor store on the way to JFK Airport, and he ended up drinking out of a bottle with some of the regulars outside the store, which I think is even funnier than the ice cream cone UL.

## *Pia Zadora heckled*

In recent years, the Golden Globes have managed to attain an aura of credibility, but that was only after a long exile from mainstream attention, during which the awards weren't even telecast. This freeze-out can be attributed largely to the fiasco of 1981, when Pia Zadora, star of *Butterfly*, won a Golden Globe as "Best New Star of the Year," much to the astonishment of anyone who had ever seen her act. The common belief was that Zadora won due to the influence of her much older producer husband, the extremely wealthy Meshulam Riklis. (When you have fewer than 100 people voting for one of five nominees, it doesn't take that much to sway an election. One can take home a statue with little more than 20 votes.)

Even as Zadora was polishing her Golden Globe, she was the subject of unrelenting humor, especially in Johnny Carson's monologues. As an attractive woman with an unusual name and a ton of chutzpah, Zadora was an easy target. No wonder she found herself headlining in an urban legend that was really nothing more than an old joke.

According to a story that still circulates to this day, Zadora's husband financed a Broadway production of *The Diary of Anne Frank*. The actress was horribly miscast as a young Jewish girl hiding from the Nazis, and the opening night crowd was barely able to contain its titters as she flung herself about the stage, drifting in and out of her accent and constantly flubbing her lines. When the Nazis arrived at her house, a jokester in the crowd couldn't resist. He stood up and said in a loud, clear voice: "She's in the attic!" Normally such boorish behavior would be met with harsh retorts, but in this case the crowd actually cheered the heckler, who walked out in triumph.

It almost sounds believable, but it never happened. Zadora has never played the role of Anne Frank, on Broadway or anywhere else.

As Zadora's name faded, I've heard the same story told about Vanna White and former Playboy Playmates Jenny McCarthy and Pamela Anderson. Needless to say, none of these blonde bombshells has ever been cast in a play about a 12-year-old Jewish girl who keeps a written record of her attempt to hide from the Nazis.

# Barbra Streisand's porno film

Rumors about big stars who made pornographic movies before they became famous have been around nearly as long as the movie industry itself. When Joan Crawford was making a name for herself in the mid-1930s, there were rumbles about a stag film in her past. According to some Hollywood historians, MGM honcho Louis B. Mayer even obtained a print, but wasn't convinced it was Crawford in the movie. Marilyn Monroe has also been mentioned as someone who did some sleazy film work before she ever got to Hollywood. I've seen a much-copied, rather blurry video purporting to show young Marilyn posing nude and rolling around for the camera. The film really isn't much more revealing than the photo shoots Marilyn participated in after she became a star.

Barbra Streisand, on the other hand, would absolutely be mortified if the world were to find out she did a hardcore porno film as a young woman. Many believe there is just such a film. This movie has been duped thousands of times and has been passed around for years on the underground circuit, always advertised as "Barbra Streisand's porno movie." There's no sound or dialogue, and the soundtrack is a cheesy, electronic type of thing, obviously added to the movie years after it was made. The black-and-white film appears to have been shot with a single camera, with a few jumps that indicate some editing was involved. For the duration of the film, we see nothing but a young couple on a sofa, engaging in sexual intercourse.

Is the girl in the movie Streisand? Well, if you were to show the movie to a friend and say, "Which Hollywood star does that woman look like?", the only possible answer would be, "Barbra Streisand." There are moments when she smiles and you're almost convinced it's really Streisand.

However, if you concentrate on her face, you begin to realize this is definitely *not* Barbra Streisand. The likely explanation is that somebody somewhere was looking at this old porno movie and noticed the resemblance to Streisand, and started circulating copies to friends, who told their friends, who told their friends, and so on. Some copies have been creatively edited to include still photos of a young Streisand so you can compare her to the porno gal—but this only serves to illustrate the differences between the two women.

Besides, if Streisand really had made such a film, there wouldn't have been that much lag time between the making of the movie and the making of Barbra Streisand, Superstar. Surely the guy who slept with the Streisand lookalike in the film, or the guy who worked the camera, or the citizens who financed the movie would have stepped forward a long time ago and said, "I know that girl!"

It never happened. Why? Because that ain't Streisand in that movie.

# *Marilyn Manson's Wonder Years*

Remember Kevin Arnold's best friend on *The Wonder Years*, Paul Pfeiffer? The kid with the big glasses and the prominent nose? Well, the geeky kid grew up to be...shock rocker Marilyn Manson! There's even an Internet site showing Paul's face morphing into Manson's, and the resemblance is pretty obvious.

Every high schooler in America has heard this one by now. It's the late 1990s version of the old "Eddie Haskell is Alice Cooper" legend that circulated a generation ago.

We seem to like to de-fang our scary rock stars. With his hateful posturing, simulated acts of violence onstage, his creepy androgynous looks, and head-pounding music, Marilyn Manson is a rather intimidating figure for some folks to ponder. But if it turns out he's just the grown-up version of that nice Paul Pfeiffer kid from *The Wonder Years*, well, now we know he's just acting, don't we?

Alas, Paul is not Marilyn, and Marilyn is not Paul. The character of Paul Pfeiffer was played by actor Josh Saviano, while Marilyn Manson was born Brian Warner in Canton, Ohio, home of the Pro Football Hall of Fame.

In a *Nick at Nite* online chat session with Saviano and fans in 1996, the very first question dealt with the Marilyn Manson story.

> Q: OK, so Josh, there is this huge rumor going around that you are Marilyn Manson. I know this isn't true, but how do you think this rumor got started and are you aware of it?

> SAVIANO: Yes, I am very much aware of it. I receive close to 20 e-mails a week asking me if this is true. Obviously it's not, but I enjoy the creativity of some people.

Fred Savage, who played Kevin Arnold on *The Wonder Years*, has also heard the rumor umpteen times. He was asked about it on E! Online.

> Q: What did you think about the rumor that Marilyn Manson was Paul from "The Wonder Years"?

> SAVAGE: More people have come up and asked me if Paul is Marilyn Manson lately than any other question. The answer is no! I'm getting a little tired of that one.

Manson's calculatedly outrageous behavior has led to several other budding urban legends: while on LSD, he lost an eye after sticking a fork in it; he throws puppies and baby ducks into the crowd at concerts and urges that the cute little animals be killed; he has raped girls on stage; he's getting breast implants; he plans to kill himself in the year 2002 with a knife shaped like a crucifix...

Wild.

# *Julia Child drops a duck*

Dan Aykroyd's imitation of Julia Child on *Saturday Night Live* was a classic. Dressed in drag, speaking in a wacky falsetto and making a mess of things in the kitchen, "Child" was unfazed by any mishaps, including the severe injuries she sustained.

Maybe it's the Aykroyd impersonation that convinced us something crazy happened in Julia Child's kitchen way back when, something that fueled the *SNL* bit. The stories abound:

Child would occasionally take a swig from a bottle of wine or cooking sherry on the air, telling viewers, "Everything tastes better if you have a little nip now and then."

Child dropped a duck on the kitchen floor, but picked it up, brushed it off, and plunked it right back in the oven. "Who's going to know?" she told viewers. "What are you going to do, throw away a perfectly good bird because you dropped it?"

In a 1995 interview with the *Chicago Tribune*, Child was asked about these rumors. "I never did [drop a duck]. People say, 'But I saw you do that.' Once, while I was flipping a potato pancake, it flipped onto the stove and I picked it up and put it back in the pan and said, 'You're alone in the kitchen.'

"It's interesting when people say, 'I saw you do it.' Or that 'I saw you pick up the bottle of wine and take a swig of it,' which I would never do."

Child said there was an incident involving a "turkey or something and it was wrapped on a counter in back of me, and it began sliding into the sink," but the turkey didn't hit the floor.

Once again, we have to remember that Julia Child's program was not live—if it were, we'd have to sit in front of the TV for hours, waiting for a goose, or turkey, or a rack of lamb to be cooked. If a turkey ever did hit the floor, or if Ms. Child had felt the urge to take a hit from a bottle of wine, they could have stopped taping and simply done another take.

## *Salute this!*

President Bill Clinton had the sorriest, sloppiest, wimpiest salute in U.S. history. Whenever Clinton encountered someone in the military, he would raise his right hand to his temple and sort of slide it out limply, with no crispness or authority whatsoever.

Let's put it this way: Gopher on the "Love Boat" had a more authoritative salute.

In his book *All Too Human*, former presidential adviser George Stephanopoulos theorized that Clinton's hesitant salute was indicative of the president's sheepishness over his own lack of military experience and the lingering perception that Clinton had aggressively dodged the draft to avoid service in Vietnam.

"He seemed to be working out his internal conflicts every time he tentatively raised his hand," wrote Stephanopoulos. "The tips of his fingers would furtively touch his slightly bowed head, as if he were being caught at something he wasn't supposed to do."

More than a few soldiers undoubtedly felt that Clinton *was* doing something he wasn't supposed to be doing. In a Feb. 15, 2001 piece, the (unabashedly conservative) *Washington Times* had a front-page story headlined, "MILITARY FINDS RE-FRESHING CHANGE WITH NEW COMMANDER-IN-CHIEF," quoting one unnamed sailor as saying, "There's been a sea change at the top. A lot of us were disgusted with President Clinton for his sexual conduct, for dodging the draft in Vietnam. President Bush, on the other hand, is one of us. And he's going to look out for us." The paper also quoted a Marine who said, "[Clinton] doesn't know us, doesn't know the first thing about us. You don't necessarily have to be in the Marines to be a good commander-in-chief, but it helps if you don't hate our guts."

The article also contrasted Bush's crisp salute with Clinton's lame efforts:

"Soldiers said Mr. Bush has the right salute, whipping his right hand so quickly that photographers often complain that they missed the picture.

"'Now that's a salute,' a 3rd Infantry Division sergeant said."

And not only does Bush snap off a better salute—he's also getting more respect than Clinton was ever accorded from the Marines, or so the story goes.

Shortly after Clinton exited the White House with his long goodbye and Bush took over, an e-mail circulated on the Internet:

I picked up on something very funny this morning. CNN showed George W. Bush leaving HM-1 [Marine One, the presidential helicopter]. The Marine at the front step saluted, Bush returned the salute, and as he walked away, the Marine executed a right face to stand facing Bush's back—something that was missing in the eight years of the Clinton presidency.

The traditional Marine Corps mark of respect was rendered to the new president. That one goes back to the days when...the Marine orderly to the ship's captain always faced him, no matter his direction of movement, to be ready to receive an order.

Who says that enlisted men can't hold back when they don't respect someone? For eight years, they did. Leave it to the Marines to speak so loudly without ever uttering a word.

It's comforting to know that the Marines are in such sync that *every single one of them* knew about this plan to dog Clinton and carried it out for two full presidential terms! I knew these guys were cogs in a lean, mean fighting machine—but this group conspiracy is truly the stuff of legend.

Urban legend, that is.

Harry Levins of the *St. Louis Post-Dispatch* tackled this story in a March 10 article, beginning with, "If the Marines disrespected Clinton, it would hurt their honor—not the president's." Levins talked to Staff Sgt. Keith Milks of the public affairs office of the Marine Corps, who said of the story: "It's absolutely false. If it were true, the Marines would see it as an insult to their honor, not to Bill Clinton. [Crew members of the presidential helicopter] are chosen for their professionalism."

When Marines and other military personnel encountered Clinton, some of them may have been thinking, "You lousy no-good draft-dodging pot-smoking womanizing intern-loving scoundrel!" but with a few exceptions, they kept a straight face and showed the proper respect to the office of the president and to their own branch of the service. As for those who didn't, e.g., Air Force Maj. Gen. Harold Campbell, who derided Clinton in public, they were reprimanded swiftly and harshly for their misconduct. Campbell's career was essentially torpedoed by his lack of respect for the president.

Clinton's exit also gave rise to a UL about the home in New York the president purchased with his wife, Hillary. Again, the ubiquitous and always unsigned e-mail was the culprit:

> Just in case your blood pressure wasn't up enough…as you know, the Clintons had to establish residence in New York for Hillary to run for the Senate. So they bought that big house—BUT there was no place for the required Secret Service agents to stay, so a special 'safe area' was built on the grounds.
>
> NOW, the Clintons are charging the Secret Service agents rent! And what a coincidence, it just so happens that the rent equals the Clintons' monthly mortgage payments! In short, we taxpayers are footing the bill for the Secret Service addition, AND the Clintons' mortgage! Such a deal, eh? What will it take for the American public to wake up? Don't you just feel like you've been suckered again, fellow taxpayers?
>
> I say let's pass this information throughout the length and the breadth of this nation to shake the American people into a heightened state of anger upon knowing they have been literally raped during their long sleep by the very trustees they have appointed to look after their interests!

First of all, nobody was "literally raped." That's a gross misuse of the term and a grossly unfair categorization of a scenario that isn't even accurate in the first place. While it is true that Secret Service agents will protect the Clintons for the remainder of their lives, the Clintons are not "charging rent" to agents. It is standard practice for the government to pay a housing fee to property owners to cover the cost of agents living on private property—but in fact the Clintons have *declined* to accept any such payments.

"They are entitled to charge [about $1,100 a month] rent, but they have decided not to do it," a White House spokesman told the New York Post.

Bill and Hillary, we salute you. With all four fingers and a thumb, that is.

## Babs avoids a land mine

Barbara Walters was in Kuwait for a report on gender roles in the Middle East for *20/20*, and she was elated to find that things has changed since her first visit to the region two decades earlier. Whereas the women used to walk several feet behind their husbands as a sign of subservience and respect, the gals were now walking several feet *ahead* of their hubbies.

Camera crew in tow, Walters approached one such woman and said, "This is so incredible! Can you tell all the millions of viewers of *20/20* how women here were able to reverse the gender roles?"

"I don't know what you mean," replied the woman.

"You used to walk behind your men, but now you're all walking ahead of them," explained Walters. "How did this change come about?"

"Oh, that," replied the woman. "Two words: land mines."

Nice to know an old joke like that can resurface as a modern urban legend, but please. First of all, where was Walters observing such behavior—on city streets? Did she stick around to see if any women got blown up in the line of wifely duty? Did she hire someone to walk ahead of herself?

The wording of the UL is also a real strong indicator that this is hokey nonsense. Are we to believe that some woman in Kuwait has the timing of Shecky Greene, with the "two words: land mines" punchline?

Four words: I don't think so.

## Celebrity shorts

Here's a quick look at some celebrity urban legends involving embarrassing incidents, secret pasts, and dubious claims. Each of these stories has been in circulation for at least a couple of years, and some have been reported as factual items in gossip columns and feature stories, but I did not uncover a single piece of evidence to lend credence to any of them.

### Fred Grandy in Congress

When Fred Grandy, who played Gopher on *The Love Boat*, was elected to the United States House of Representatives, he had a predictably difficult time gaining the respect of the cynical, jaded types on Capitol Hill. Everyone was snickering about "Congressman Gopher"—even though Grandy was a dedicated, intelligent, well-informed fellow.

On the day Grandy was sworn in, he entered an elevator already crowded with a number of congressmen and senators. He could see the knowing glances and the smirking smiles starting to form on some faces; he knew they were thinking, "Hey look, it's Gopher!"

As the elevator doors closed, the congressional page who was operating the elevator turned to Grandy and said, "Lido Deck, sir?"

Everyone burst into laughter, but Grandy didn't think it was funny. He grabbed the page's credentials and ID and had the young man fired. From that point on, people realized it wasn't a good idea to joke with Fred Grandy about his television past.

## Unlikely snipers

At least two celebrities with benign images have been "outed" as being former sharpshooters. The grandfatherly Dave Thomas of the Wendy's hamburger chain was alleged to have been in the National Guard, and was one of the troops deployed to Kent State University on May 4, 1970—the day four students were gunned down by National Guardsmen. Thomas supposedly was the one who fired the first shot, a decision that haunts him to this very day and keeps Wendy's PR people awake at night, wondering when some enterprising journalist is going to uncover the story.

Another former military man was the late John Henry Deutchendorff, better known to his millions of fans as John Denver. In the late 1960s, Denver was stationed in Vietnam as a highly trained sniper, and his technique was so legendary it was called "The Denver Method." Denver would hide out in a tree with the sun in a certain position behind him, wait for his prey to come into range; and make a low whistling noise to get their attention. When they'd look up, they'd be momentarily blinded by the sun, and Denver would open fire. Using this method, he killed dozens of Vietcong and was decorated with a ton of medals.

Only after returning to the States and raising his consciousness did Denver feel haunted by what he'd done in Vietnam. He threw away his medals, tore up his commendations, took up the guitar, and embraced a passive lifestyle—but he couldn't totally lose the memories of his years as a sniper. In fact, one of Denver's biggest feel-good hits was a tacit admission of his dark past. "Sunshine on My Shoulders" might have sounded like a sappy little ballad, but in reality, Denver was confronting his 'Nam alter ego, the sniper who waited in the trees for the sunlight to blind his enemies so he could extinguish their lives: "Sunshine on my shoulders, makes me happy..."

Only problem is, John Denver never served in Vietnam. In the 1960s he was already pursuing a musical career.

## Leann Rimes' real age

Unlike other teenage singing sensations, Leann Rimes has always sounded like a grown woman. Her mature phrasing and robust vocals seemed incongruous coming from a 14-year-old girl, which has led to some Internet speculation that she was more like 18 or 20 when she hit the scene. Nonsense.

Y‌ou're not going to believe what happened to me when I finished this book. I decided to celebrate the completion of the job, so I went to the fridge to see if there was anything cold and refreshing available. Oh that's right! I had a six-pack of Miller Genuine Draft chilling—and the best thing about it was, it didn't cost me a nickel. See, to celebrate the millennium, Miller's been giving away coupons good for a free six-pack of any of their fine beer products.[1] All you have to do is respond to the e-mail message that's been making the rounds. It's easy!

As I sipped my free beer, I clicked on the TV and started channel-surfing. An old episode of "Leave it to Beaver" was on. That used to be one of my favorite shows, but now it's just too depressing to watch, knowing that the Beaver died in Vietnam and Eddie Haskell became a porn star who died of AIDS.[2,3] I clicked over to a showing of *Goldfinger* on cable, but that was upsetting, too. That poor woman covered in gold paint suffocated to death,[4] and no one knew it as they were filming the scene! What a tragedy. I clicked to another station, and there was the actress Jamie Lee Curtis on a talk show. Looking at her in that tight outfit, you'd never guess she was born a hermaphrodite.[5]

Just then the phone rang. It was my friend Bob, asking me if I'd checked my e-mail messages in the last hour. When I told him I hadn't, Bob said, "Well, make sure you do before you go to bed tonight. There's a sick little girl named Jessica Mydek who needs our help,[6] and I also included that secret recipe for Mrs. Field's Cookies I was telling you about.[7] Plus I finally found Kurt Vonnegut's great commencement speech from a few years ago,[8] I think you'll find some valuable life lessons in there."

"Can't wait to access all that valuable information," I told my friend. "So what did you do tonight?"

"I rented a video, but I got more than I bargained for," he told me. "When I popped the tape in my VCR, all of a sudden there's this couple just going at it like crazy. I guess when they returned the video to the store, they left the movie at home and put one of their amateur sex tapes in the box[9]!"

"The strangest things happen to you," I said. "Like when you tried to buy that 'hot' VCR, and you came home and found out the box had nothing but bricks in it."[10]

"You're telling me. Oh man, look at the time, I've gotta go! I've got a date with a nurse who was working in the emergency room the night they brought Travolta in with that sausage taped to his leg!"[11]

"You're one lucky guy," I said. "Good night."

I hung up the phone, just as my girlfriend Marisa Tomei[12] walked in.

"I've made a decision," she said.

"I'm giving back the Oscar."[13]

If you believed any of that—especially the part about Marisa Tomei being my girlfriend—you must have decided to read this book from back to front. Any amateur urban legendologist could have spotted a dozen UL's in the preceding story.

Which brings us to the next chapter, or chapters. The 100 or so too-good-to-be-true-tales discussed in this book represent only a small portion of the stories out there. With your help, I plan to continue chronicling urban legends in the years to come. Please feel free to contact me with your favorite urban legends—the fresher the better, no hook-in-the-car-door stories, please.

The *X-Files* has it wrong; the truth *isn't* out there. It's my mission to see that this changes.

Richard Roeper

Write me c/o:   The Chicago Sun-Times
401 N. Wabash
Chicago, IL, 60611

Fax:   312-321-2120
E-mail:   rroeper@suntimes.com

---

[1] Urban legend.
[2,3] Urban legend, urban legend.
[4] UL.
[5] Another UL.
[6] An urban legend.
[7] Ibid.
[8] Ibid, ibid, ibid. (Sounds kinda like a frog, doesn't it?)
[9] You know it, you love it, you can't live without it: Another urban legend.
[10] UL.
[11] Yep. Urban legend.
[12] Folks, this ain't an urban legend. It's a pathetic male fantasy.
[13] UL.

The two best urban legend sites on the Internet are:
    "Urban Legends Reference Page," *snopes.com*
    The urban legend site at *about.com*

## The Classics
**"They're stealing our kidneys!"**
New Orleans Police Dept. notice. Reprinted with permission.

**Dog swallows cell phone**
Story reprinted with permission from the *London Sun*.

**The truth about Furbys**
Interview, Tiger Electronics, March 1999.
Vernon Loeb, "A Toy Story of Hairy Espionage; NSA Bans
    Furby From Spy Agency's Premises," *Washington Post*,
    January 13, 1999, p. A21.

**Gang initiation rites**
Dear Abby column, "Better Shop Around For Well-Policed
    Malls," *Chicago Tribune*, April 23, 1992, p. 17

**Tainted needles**
Michael Sluss, "Urban Myth Is Reality," *The Roanoke Times*,
    February 11, 1999, p. B83
Michael Sluss, "Third Needle Incident is Reported in
    Pulaski," *The Roanoke Times*, February 12, 1999, p. 2

**The Gerber rebate**
Statement from Gerber Co. Reprinted with permission.

**Craig Shergold's dying wish**
Interview with Michelle Lewis, Public Relations Executive with Make-A-Wish Foundation, March 1999.

**"Are You Gay?"**
Information from USAir obtained from author interview with USAir director of public relations David Castlevetter, March 1999.

**"Good Luck, Mr. Gorsky"**
Interview with NASA's Director of Media Services, Brian Welch, April 1999.
NASA transcripts. Reprinted with permission.

**Toothbrush bandits**
Wallace, David Foster, *Infinite Jest*, Little Brown and Company, February 1996, p. 55

**Legends of Rolling Rock**
Rege Behe, "Rolling Rock: A 12-Ouncer Takes an Incredible Journey," *Pittsburgh Tribune-Review*, Aug. 31, 1997.

**"Welcome to the world of AIDS"**
Interview with CDC's HIV Media Specialist, Kitty Bina, March 1999.

**Flight 261 stopped in mid-prayer**
Richard Jerome, and Berestein, Leslie. "Keeping hope alive; his parents killed on Alaska Airlines Flight 261, Jeff Knight refuses to let their life's mission die with them." *People*, May 22, 2000, p. 58.
James Wallace. "Flight 261 prayer story spreads via e-mail." *Seattle Post-Intelligencer*, April 3, 2000, p. B3.
James Wallace. "Flight 261 pilots struggled to the end; NTSB opens day of hearings on crash of Flight 261." *Seattle Post-Intelligencer,* Dec. 14, 2000, p. A1.
Gina Piccalo, and Gorman, Anna. "The crash of Flight 261." *Los Angeles Times*, Feb. 9, 2000, p. 1.

Air traffic control transcript excerpts, Alaska Airlines Flight 261, Jan. 31, 2000.

**George Turklebaum, we hardly knew ye**

Dave Murphy. "On the fringe." *San Francisco Chronicle*, May 4, 2001, p. B5.

"Worker dead at desk for 5 days." *Birmingham Sunday Mercury* Dec. 17, 2000, p. 9.

Martin Waller. "Overtime." *The London Times*, Jan. 11, 2001, Business section.

Martin Waller. "Dead useful." *The London Times*, May 9, 2001, Business section.

Rodney Rothman. "My Fake Job." *The New Yorker*, Nov. 27, 2000, p. 120.

Jonathan Bing. "New Yorker 'Fake Job' story really is bogus." *Daily Variety*, Dec. 6, 2000, p. 5.

Gabriel Snyder, and Gay, Jason, and Goldman, Andrew. "Dot.com spy's virtual journalism makes big trouble at New Yorker." *New York Observer*, Dec. 11, 2000.

Bettijane Levine. "Here at the New Yorker, a literary imbroglio." *Los Angeles Times*, Jan. 21, 2001, Living section, p. 2.

## Big Lies on Campus

**Psychic predicts massacre**

Jeff Ristine, "At USD, Massacre Rumor Means Harrowing Halloween," *San Diego Union-Tribune*, October 31, 1998, p. 1B.

Scott Powers, "Legend Haunting College Campuses," *The Columbus (Ohio) Dispatch*, October 31, 1998, p. 5C.

**Porn 'n' Chicken**

Stein joel, "A StaXXX session." *New York Observer*, Nov. 27, 2000.

"The chicken was delicious." *Time*, May 7, 2001, p. 21.

"Media swallows Yale porn hoax." *New York Post*, March 11, 2001, p. 10.

Tristan Taormino. "Porn, chicken and boy toys." *The Village Voice*, March 6, 2001, p. 148.

Ben Figa. "Yale student group Porn 'n' Chicken produces porn film. *Daily Northwestern*, Feb. 13, 2001.

*London Evening Standard.* "Yale students prove they have naked ambition; Ivy League's finest are making porn film." Jan. 31, 2001, p. 27.

Author e-mail exchanges with Porn 'n' Chicken

## Legends of the Silver Screen

### The munchkin suicide

The Straight Dope, Cecil Adams, May 1997.

Leslie Doolittle, "Really Most Sincerely, Still a Munchkin," by Leslie *Orlando Sentinel*, October 29, 1996, p. A2.

### The Marisa Tomei Oscar mistake

Roger Ebert, "The Answer Man," Showcase Section, *Chicago Sun-Times*, June 15, 1997, p. 5.

"And the Loser Is: Bad Oscar Rumor," *The Hollywood Reporter*, March 22, 1994.

David Sheehan, "For Outstanding Achievement in the Art of Oscar Rumors," *Orange County Register*, March 29, 1994, p. F2.

### The *Twister* tornado

Mark Steyn, "A Nobody in My Neck of the Woods," *London Daily Telegraph*, May 24, 1996, p. 26.

### Legends of *Titanic*

Patrick Goldstein, "'Doctor Zzzhivago?' Many of This Season's Releases Have Epic Lengths, but That Doesn't Always Reflect Epic Visions," Calendar Section, *The Los Angeles Times*, December 4, 1997.

*Good Morning America* transcripts, December 31, 1997 and January 15, 1998.

### Disney's secret messages

*Movie Guide*, March, 1995.

Lisa Bannon, "How a Rumor Spread About Subliminal Sex in Disney's 'Aladdin,' " *The Wall Street Journal*, October 24, 1995, p. A1.

David Koenig, *Mouse Under Glass: Secrets of Disney Animation and Theme Parks*, Bonaventure Press, 1997.

## Lawfully Wedded Legends
### The philandering groom
*Bold and the Beautiful*, April 1999. Information reprinted with permission

## Rumors "In the Air Tonight"
### A killer "In the Air Tonight"
"Walter Scott's Personality Parade." *Parade*, September 27, 1992.

### J. Lo gets the heave-ho
"Laugh? I nearly got the sack." *London Guardian*. June 5, 2001, p. 16.

Beth Keil, Landman, and Spiegelman, Ian. "A Lopez hoax goes global." *Intelligener, newyorkmag.com*, June 11, 2001.

Andrew Ross Sorkin. "An e-mail boast to friends puts executive out of work." *New York Times*, May 22, 2001, Section C, p. 2.

"J. Lo (Jennifer Lopez) takes 'diva' to a new level. "*Buzzle.com*. May 2, 2001.

"Hell hath no fury like J. Lo's magical butt." *iFilm.com*. Hollywood e-mail, May 16, 2001.

### "You Oughta Know" who this song's about
John Sakamato, "Hell Hath No Fury Like Alanis Scorned," *Toronto Sun*, July 6, 1995.

### Other chart-topping legends
Achy Obejas "Manson Madness,"*Chicago Tribune*, Feb. 19, 1999, P. 3, Section 5.

## Cybermyths and Other Online Gossip

**Audrey Hepburn's beauty tips**

Luz Sapin Micabalo. "For lovely girls, our 'beauty tips.'" *Filipino Reporter*, Jan. 18, 2001, p. 22.

Trish Donnally. "This beauty shares her tips." *San Francisco Chronicle*, Jan. 27, 1992, p. D5.

Jim Kelly. "Writing is an integral part of Bucks woman's life." Allentown (Pa.) *Morning Call*, May 12, 1999, p. B2.

Yahoo! Biographies of Audrey Hepburn and Sam Levinson.

**The virtual death of Kaycee Nicole**

Katie Hafner. "A beautiful life, an early death, a fraud exposed." *New York Times,* May 31, 2001, Section G, p. 1.

Dianne Lynch. "Not dead." *ABCnews.com,* May 30, 2001.

Jackson, Ron. "Victim puts face on hoax." *Daily Oklahoman,* May 24, 2001.

van der Woning, Ryan. "The end of the whole mess." Internet posting, May, 30, 2001.

"FBI will not pursue Internet hoax." AP Online, May 31, 2001.

**"The Paradox of Our Time"**

"Tears and blame at hearing on guns." *Seattle Post-Intelligencer*. May, 28, 1999, p. A3.

Ken Foskett. "Gore accuses GOP of bowing on guns." *Atlanta Journal and Constitution*, May 28, 1999, Metro edition.

CBS News Transcripts, May 28, 1999. "Parents of the victims of the Columbine High School shootings take their case to Congress and the courts."

CNN "Talkback Live." May 28, 1999.

Michael Romano. "Columbine victim's dad says NRA a scapegoat." *Denver Rocky Mountain News*, May 28, 1999, p. 4A.

David Lightman. "Amid rhetoric about gun laws, a father speaks." *Hartford Courant*, May 28, 1999, p. A14.

Rev. Cedric Broughton. "Change from within is what
counts." *Lewiston Morning Tribune*, June 12, 1999, p. 13A.

Lewis W. Diuguid. "E-mail offers provocative paradoxes to
ponder." *Kansas City Star*, June 24, 1999, Southland section,
p. 1.

Hacks-R-Us homepage: *firstamo.com/hacksrus.htm*

**Nike shoe rebate**
Quote from company statement. Reprinted with permission.

**Blacks losing the right to vote**
Statement from Dept. of Justice. Reprinted with permission.

paul Shepard "Online Hoax Prods Black Leaders Into
Action," *Associated Press*, December 2, 1998.

**Shannon's Internet lesson**
Interview with Bill Guillet, spokesman for Canton, N.C.
Police Dept., March 1999.

## Tall Tales of the Rich and Famous

**Richard Gere and the gerbil**
*Palm Beach Post*, September 5, 1995.

**Mariah Carey's callous remark**
A.J. Benza, "The Skinny on Mariah Hoax," *New York Daily
News*, September 11, 1996, p. 24.

**Tiger Woods at the strip club**
*Milwaukee Journal*, October 20, 1996.

Steve Rosenbloom, "Foulline," Sports Section, *Chicago
Tribune*, October 28, 1996, p. 2.

**Tommy Hilfiger unfairly maligned**
Mimi Avins, "Take a Spin Inside Tommy Hilfiger's Fashion
Cuisinart," *The Los Angeles Times Magazine* section, August
25, 1996, p. 19.

Statement from Tommy Hilfiger. Reprinted with permission.

**Keanu Reeves marries David Geffen**
Tim Allis, "Keanu Sets the Record Straight," *Out*, July/
August, 1995, P. 65, 116-117.

**Marilyn Manson's** *Wonder Years*
Transcript from E! Online Web site. Reprinted with permission.

**Julia Child drops a duck**
by Alan Solomon "Queen of Cuisine: Julia Child Continues to Reign Over the Hearts of Her Fans," *Chicago Tribune*, May 10, 1995, P. 7, Section 2.

**Salute this!**
Lloyd Grove. "The Reliable Source." *Washington Post*, Jan. 12, 2001, Style section, p. 3.
"Bill passes up Secret Service $$." *New York Post*, Jan. 16, 2001, p. 10.
Joseph Curl. "Military finds refreshing change with new commander in chief." *Washington Times*, Feb. 15, 2001, p. A1.
Harry Levins. "Don't believe your e-mail; the Marines didn't show more respect to Bush than Clinton." *St. Louis Post-Dispatch*, March 10, 2001, p. 2.

# Index

# About the Author

Richard Roeper is the co-host of the nationally syndicated *Ebert & Roeper and the Movies*. Roeper also writes a daily general interest column for the *Chicago Sun-Times*, which is distributed nationally by the New York Times Syndicate. He has won two Chicago/Midwest Emmys for his television commentaries on the Fox affiliate in Chicago, and he has hosted radio programs on a number of Chicago stations. He lives in Chicago.